COACH CHESTNUT'S URBAN SURVIVOR NOTES

REAL LIFE, REAL SOLUTIONS, RAW EMOTIONS, APPLICABLE ACTIONS

VOLUME 1

COACH CHESTNUT'S URBAN SURVIVOR NOTES

REAL LIFE, REAL SOLUTIONS, RAW EMOTIONS, APPLICABLE ACTIONS

VOLUME 1

COACH DEMONE A CHESTNUT

Ordering Information:

Orders by U.S. trade bookstores and wholesalers. Quantity sales. Special discounts are available on quantity purchases by corporations, associations, and others. For details, contact the publisher at the following email address:

Connect with DeMone A. Chestnut

Email:
iamcoachchestnut@gmail.com

For merchandise and apparel go to www.coachchestnut.com or www.peaytown.com.

Instagram:
Instagram.com/iamcoachchestnut

Facebook:
Facebook.com/demone.chestnut

LinkedIn:
LinkedIn.com/in/coachchestnut

YouTube:
https://www.youtube.com/channel/UCpbtpdyIe-MvCBB4fan-C2Og/featured

ISBN: 979-8-9859780-0-1

ACKNOWLEDGMENTS

First, I would like to thank God for allowing me to remain on earth to serve and giving me grace when I was not deserving.

Thank you to the city of Buffalo, NY and all my close friends and family from the Commodore Perry Projects, Shaffer Village Projects, Millicent Townhomes, Humber Avenue residents, Butler Avenue residents, Cool Springs, Bailey & Kensington Crew. I AM YOU!

Thank you to the Clarksville-Montgomery County community for helping me grow into manhood, raise my kids, and become a professional coach, educator, soldier, and investigator.

Thank you to all my Thomas A. Sims Lodge #170, Aviano, Italy AB & Fort Campbell comrades I appreciate your love and kindness. We will forever be connected.

Much respect to the Ali, Holloway, Patterson, O'Neal, Lipscomb, Middlebrook, Culverhouse, Bird, Farrell, Reed, Henry, Alwakeel, Mathis, Carter, Jackson, Hartley, Cunningham, Bell, Watkins, Chandler, Stubbs, Boyd, Martin, Haskins, Cook, Webb, Johnson, Wells, Williford, Kumiyama, Akama, Herrera, Henderson, Angel, Crouthamel, De Leon, Paddock, Woodruff, Wiroll, Hill, Gomez, Jones, Mendez, Harrison, Russell, Vicari, Green, Pugh, Brannon, Chapman, Slight, Dove, Holt, Demps, MEG & B, Lindsey, Daniels, Wolff, Ms. Paola, Marshall, Freeman, Rundel, Post, Wilson, Fitting, Garrett, Wilens, Leaverton,

Gamble, Jennings, Shufford, Gordon, Harris, Barrett, Hugley, Norfleet, Ulrey, Pride, Haugabook, Wood, Simon, Leon, Parkes, Meeks, Boone, Boykin, Thomas, Eric Todd, Huhnke, Jemison, Barnes, Coffey, Verlene, Pitts, Padula, Hollifield, Ken Haynes, Rutledge, Lovelock, Sensabaugh, Figueroa, Taylor, Burroughs, and Glover families.

To all my brothers, sisters, nieces, nephews, cousins, aunts, uncles, in-laws I really appreciate every word of encouragement spoken and written about me; your support means the world to me.

Lyric Brooks, Caitlin Cox Duncan, Lori Taylor, Dr. Chiquita S. Jackson, DaDawn Taylor, and Maceo D.L. Chestnut: thank you for your contribution to this manuscript.

Sharee Moore with Dynasty Self-Publishing Services, thank you for your patience and bringing my idea to life.

CONTENTS

INTRODUCTION xi
NOTE #1 YOUR NAME IS YOUR BRAND 1
NOTE #2 MUSIC CALMS THE SAVAGE BEAST 3
NOTE #3 BODY LANGUAGE 5
NOTE #4 VOCABULARY KEEPS YOU VITAL 6
NOTE #5 CULTURE IS COMMON, NOT CRITICAL 8
NOTE #6 IDENTITY IS SELF-CARE 9
NOTE #7 NICENESS IS NEEDED 10
NOTE #8 SAVE SOME MONEY 13
NOTE #9 INVEST 14
NOTE #10 CHANGE IS A CHALLENGE 16
NOTE #11 THE DOG IN YOU 17
NOTE #12 ZIP CODES AND AREA CODES 18
NOTE #13 GIRL POWER 20
NOTE #14 KARMA IS CONTAGIOUS 23
NOTE #15 PASSION MAY BE YOUR PURPOSE 25
NOTE #16 PURPOSE DICTATES YOUR INTENTION 26
NOTE #17 GOALS 27
NOTE #18 CHALLENGES OF A STROLLER 28
NOTE #19 MOTO THE MIND 29
NOTE #20 PERCEPTIONS x2 31
NOTE #21 LIVE FEARLESSLY 32
NOTE #22 LEADERS LEAD FROM THE FRONT, NOT THE REAR 33
NOTE #23 LOVE 34
NOTE #24 REALITY COMES AT YOU FAST 37

NOTE #25 CONFIDENCE IS NO COINCIDENCE 38
NOTE #26 VALUE 40
NOTE #27 VIBES AND ENERGY 41
NOTE #28 BE RESOURCEFUL. DON'T GIVE UP. 42
NOTE #29 LOVE SOUNDS LIKE AND LOOKS LIKE LOVE 43
NOTE #30 WHEN IN DOUBT 44
NOTE #31 JUST BECAUSE YOU MADE IT DOES NOT MEAN YOU'RE DONE 45
NOTE #32 FEELINGS 46
NOTE #33 MOTIVATION IS TEMPORARY 47
NOTE #34 LOYALTY IS LIMITED 48
NOTE #35 INTUITION MUST BE TESTED BEFORE IT CAN BE TRUSTED 49
NOTE #36 CLICHÉS 50
NOTE #37 TRAVEL 51
NOTE #38 SUICIDE 53
NOTE #39 FRIEND 55
NOTE #40 PARENTS 56
NOTE #41 BE WITH PEOPLE ENTHUSIASTICALLY 57
NOTE #42 KNOW YOUR RIGHTS 60
NOTE #43 DECISIONS 61
NOTE #44 VICES 62
NOTE #45 IN THE ZONE 63
NOTE #46 COMPLIMENTS 65
NOTE #47 KNOW THE DIFFERENCE BETWEEN THE 3 C'S 66
NOTE #48 UNDERSTAND THE IMPORTANCE OF AUNTS AND UNCLES 68
NOTE #49 CURVE THEM LIKE THEY CURVE YOU 69
NOTE #50 JUST BECAUSE YOU'RE WORKING HARD DOES NOT MEAN YOU'RE WORKING EFFICIENTLY 70
NOTE #51 DREAM 72
NOTE #52 CHEAT CODE 73
NOTE #53 POWER COLOR 74
NOTE #54 BOOKS BUILD MINDS 75
NOTE #55 MULTITASKING MAKES IT MESSY 76
NOTE #56 INSPIRATIONAL RESPONSIBILITY 77

NOTE #57 TAXES.....78
NOTE #58 SEX.....80
NOTE #59 DISTRACTIONS.....82
NOTE #60 PROCRASTINATION STOPS PROGRESSION..83
NOTE #61 DRUGS.....84
NOTE #62 HUGS ARE POWERFUL.....86
NOTE #63 THE PIVOT.....87
NOTE #64 HATE - HURT - HONOR.....89
NOTE #65 RULES ARE MERELY GUIDELINES.....90
NOTE #66 CLOSED MOUTHS DON'T GET FED.....91
NOTE #67 HURT, NOT HATE.....92
NOTE #68 NEW YOU, NEW ME.....93
NOTE #69 FLAWS AND FREEDOM.....95
NOTE #70 "QUIT MOMENT".....96
NOTE #71 MAINTAIN YOUR STANDARDS.....97
NOTE #72 FORESIGHT.....98
NOTE #73 PROGRESSION OVER PERFECTION.....99
NOTE #74 YOUR GIFT.....100
NOTE #75 A GOOD LIFE IS EXPENSIVE.....101
NOTE #76 BEING A PARENT IS NOT A LIFESTYLE.....102
NOTE #77 SUPPLY DICTATES DEMAND.....103
NOTE #78 EXCLUSIVITY RAISES THE VALUE.....104
NOTE #79 YOU CAN'T SAVE EVERYONE.....105
NOTE #80 CONSTRUCTIVE CRITICISM BUILDS CHARACTER.....106
NOTE #81 YOUR LIFESTYLE VS. YOUR CAREER.....107
NOTE #82 MAKE YOUR OWN LANE.....108
NOTE #83 COUNT ON YOURSELF!.....109
NOTE #84 MOST REWARDING JOBS WILL COST TIME AND NOT PAY WELL.....110
NOTE #85 MOMENTS IN THE MOMENT.....111
NOTE #86 QUALITY YOU CAN AFFORD.....112
NOTE #87 WINNERS . . . WIN.....113
NOTE #88 BE DANGEROUS.....114
NOTE #89 GO TO WEDDINGS.....115
NOTE #90 OLD STANDARDS VS. NEW BEGINNINGS.....116
NOTE #91 RACE CARD.....117
NOTE #92 PROCRASTINATION.....118
NOTE #93 FIRE.....119

NOTE #94 DOLLA BILL 120
NOTE #95 G.I. 121
NOTE #96 HOOD LOVE 122
NOTE #97 BEGGING 123
NOTE #98 STEPPARENTS 124
NOTE #99 HEROES 126
EPILOGUE 129

INTRODUCTION

The purpose of this blueprint is to provide fundamental tactics and techniques for young adults in need of guidance to survive in an urban environment. This information may also serve as a refresher for the more experienced urban dwellers. More importantly, this blueprint was inspired by my children, Sadaija and Maceo Chestnut, and all my former students and athletes who attended West Creek High School in Tennessee. My life mission is to empower youth, and what better way to do that than by providing a blueprint so that they can better prepare themselves for life outside the classroom and off the playing field?

As you migrate through the survival notes, you will notice that I follow a pattern. I'm offering a piece of advice, followed by an experience or incident to support that advice. Also included are music titles that were either playing in the background or inspired me as I wrote ***Coach Chestnut's Urban Survivor Notes***. Music feeds and motivates me, and I hope it does the same for you.

This manuscript does not pose all the questions one might ask, nor does it provide all the answers, but it sets the foundation. This work is listed as volume one, which alludes to more to follow, such as workshops, life coaching services, and speaking engagements. As mentioned before, empowering youth is my lifelong mission, and I'm committed to it. Furthermore, I know this work will last long after I'm gone. It's my legacy; the dash between the day I was born and the day I die. This book documents the many times that I have fallen and gotten back up even more determined.

I believe this work will also serve as evidence that the time my parents and all those who invested in me was not wasted. In many ways, I'm carrying the torch once held by my grandmother, Emma Jane Savage, who fostered hundreds of children in the city of Buffalo, NY. My mother, Shirley D. Webb-Hall, and godmother, Gertie Graham, were life-long social workers and consumer advocates. This work also challenges my own children to take the baton – to not just exist, but to be present and give back to society no matter how unfair it may be at times. This work challenges every student and athlete I've ever coached to go get their future and also be humble and give back to the community that served them as well!

LEAD OR BE LED.

My notes are not typical textbook subject matters, nor are my experiences. However, I'm candid and honest in my experiences without making my friends and family members feel exposed or betrayed. I am not ashamed of my life's journey, nor of anyone who was along for the ride. Many incidents that most youth and young adults find themselves experiencing are captured in this work. How do I know what I'm talking about? Because I *listen* to the youth so that I can empower them. The source of my information also comes from personal experiences, trials, tribulations, wins, and losses. Preparation came from being the youngest of thirteen children, eight years in the military, fourteen years as a police officer, twenty-one years coaching track/cross country teams, and eight years as an educator, and failed relationships.

I've played many roles in my life, such as star athlete, womanizer, main dude, side dude, friend, friend with benefits, sneaky link, jumpoff, criminal, leader, witness, and victim. In life, I cheated on women and have been cheated on by women. I took it on the chin like a champ, too. I learned to embrace my karma at a young age. At age fifteen, I was doing strong-arm robberies (snatch and grabs), was sexually active by age twelve, stole cars so I could drive to adult clubs, I was suspended from school every year from fifth grade to the week of graduation during my senior year of high school. In fact, I had a parent-teacher conference just hours prior to graduation to determine if I would be able to walk across the stage with my peers. I consumed alcoholic beverages and dated students from Buffalo State College while I was enrolled at Lewis J. Bennett High School. Surprisingly, just like many of today's youth and young adults, I flew under the radar because I had decent grades, played sports all year round, and worked two jobs.

A special thank you to the mothers of my children, Geneva R. Sharpley (mother of Sadaija) and Michelle A. Martin (mother of Maceo). Both of my children's mothers had a relationship with my parents outside of me, and for that, I am truly grateful. As I became unraveled and reclusive after the deaths of both of my parents, Michelle held it down for me. I am thankful and humbled by her kindness and loyalty.

This blueprint is dedicated to my godmother, Mrs. Gertie Graham, my grandmother, Mrs. Emma Jane Keeve-Savage, my mother, Shirley Webb-Hall aka "Shaw," and my father, friend, and road dog, Clyde J. Chestnut.

Respectfully,
DeMone A. Chestnut
"The Urban Survivor"

YOUR NAME IS YOUR BRAND

When you meet and greet people, make sure you say your name with confidence, pride, and enthusiasm. Get your chin up, put your chest out, project your voice, and use clear pronunciation.

This is by far the first message you send when you want respect without asking for it. Your name is your brand, just like Nike, Gucci, and Adidas. Acknowledge that you, too, can be a Fortune 500 company. Sell and market your brand every chance you get; this increases your value monetarily and culturally.

This is a must whether you come from money or have never seen real money. Be definitive and let your brand stand out on its merit.

While playing high school sports and serving in the United States Army, I quickly noticed that, when your name is called, a vibe and energy supersedes your response and arrival. People wonder what will be said once you are dead and gone. Well, I believe it will be the same thing that is said in your absence and upon your arrival when you're expected. Being a law enforcement detective, I had to make sure I promoted my name, brand, and skill set regularly because the demographics illustrated that it was rare to find someone who looks like me in the rooms that I wanted to occupy. As the positive, respectful persona of law enforcement officers declined, I quickly and strategically pivoted to the title of "Coach Chestnut." My name and brand had to be protected; I worked too hard for too long to allow it to be compromised. My work and passion to empower youth is too important, so I had to preserve my integrity.

VIBE

Prince – **"Call My Name"**
Big Pun – **"It's So Hard"**

MUSIC CALMS THE SAVAGE BEAST

Music is the most constant art form that can mend emotional, racial, and gender barriers.

Deep, deep, deep down inside, I'm a hopeless romantic, but I don't communicate well in relationships. I've always used music to help get my point across, but even that gets misconstrued. I can assure you that trying to send music or messages with the right tone is important, and hopefully the person the message is intended for is in the right mood to receive it. The fear of them taking the lyrics literally or interpreting the title without the right context is real. More importantly, will they listen to the lyrics at all? So many of my specially cultivated playlists have fallen on deaf ears, cold hearts, and blind eyes. My goal with music was to use it as a conduit in hopes of softening the message, heightening my effort, personalizing the point I wanted to deliver. Generally speaking, if you're the one who's at fault, or the other person just doesn't want to speak to you, maybe they're willing to listen to music provided to them. This shows some effort to make things right. But if the person you're dealing with is extremely critical, this could backfire.

Music feeds many segments of me as a person. It's nutrition without physical consumption, my vitamin B-12, D, and C. It fuels me, humbles me, drives me, and motivates me. I'm committed to music.

VIBE

Lee Fields – ***"Don't Leave Me This Way"***
Joe Budden - **"Love, I'm Good"**
Leela James – "**Complicated"**

BODY LANGUAGE

Your body language speaks louder than words. You must be aware of your body language. For example, I had to learn to smile and develop a poker face because my careers as a homicide investigator, child sex abuse investigator, and high school track & field coach demanded it. Children who had survived sexual abuse didn't need my sourpuss facial expression. This took effort because I wasn't the type of person who walked around smiling. I frowned a lot and didn't even know it. That was the wrong message; I was not approachable. So, to level the playing field, I smiled and became approachable when needed. For my fellas, don't feel as though you have to suppress your masculinity for that to happen because that's not the case. Just be aware of your body language and the messages being sent in certain situations. The sucking of your teeth, rolling of your eyes, folding of your arms, looking away during a conversation are all bad juju. These actions can impact your employment, progress, business, and ability to get to know and meet people who can change the trajectory of your life.

VIBE

Beyonce & Kanye West – "**Ego**"
Run DMC – "**King of Rock**"

VOCABULARY KEEPS YOU VITAL

Vocabulary is key to growth, especially if you're not an avid reader.

My mother was big on reading at a young age, but I was not. Once she realized that I was not going to conform to cranking out new novels every month, she started "words of the week," which, for me, was just as bad as eating brussels sprouts. My mother started on page one of the biggest dictionary I had ever seen in my life. In my eyes, it was equivalent to a New York City telephone book. "Shaw," as she was affectionately known, made me define the word, use the word in a sentence, then tell a story using the word. This was in addition to my actual daily schoolwork and homework. In my opinion, this was equivalent to the nuns at the school I attended, All Saints Catholic School, stepping on my baby toe as a form of discipline.

However, I can't tell you how many times my deep vocabulary has saved me academically and socially. To this day, I've only shared with my students in the Criminal Justice and Homeland Security Academy that I have dyslexia. My mother never fed into my "issue" so that I wouldn't allow it to be a crutch. All assessment results of my disability were discarded immediately, like cigarette butts.

Writing has always been a weakness of mine, but I knew I'd still pen this manuscript. This, in itself, is my testimony, confidence builder, and a testimony to my desire to EMPOWER YOUTH!

VIBE

Tupac – "**Dear Mama**"
Kanye w/ Jay-Z – "**Never Let Me Down**"

CULTURE IS COMMON, NOT CRITICAL

You cannot allow family, friends, associates, and cultural norms dictate what you can and cannot do.

If you're African American and want to play hockey, then play damn hockey. If you want to go whitewater rafting or skydiving, do these things. If you want to be a police officer or join the military, do it. If you're from the North and want to move to the South or live out West, then pack your bags and hit the road, Jack. Do what life is calling you to do. Bet on yourself every time. Don't allow insecurities from your cultural norms to stunt your growth. Do not allow others or your family dynamics to stop you from progressing and growing into the person that you're destined to be.

VIBE

Kanye West - **"Can't Tell Me Nothing"**
Ray Charles – **"Hit the Road Jack"**

IDENTITY IS SELF-CARE

You must first identify yourself as an individual within the culture you come from.

Some cultures will tell you things that you shouldn't do. You shouldn't wear those colors. You shouldn't wear this jacket or that dress. You shouldn't drive this type of car. At one time, if a women wore red lipstick, it was predetermined that she was a prostitute. On more than one occasion, I was told, "You do white people stuff." I knew what they meant, but I didn't care. Who you become and what you want out of life are your responsibilities. At the end of the day, good or bad, rich or poor, it is still your life. Define the type of life you want to live, then spend the rest of your time cultivating it.

VIBE

Yo Gotti – **"More Ready Than Ever"**
Joe Budden – **"Only Human"**

NICENESS IS NEEDED

I get it . . . In this world, it's difficult to be nice. Do it anyway. Don't be a doormat. But be nice. It feels good, trust me. My mother was a stern woman, no doubt about that. As a social worker, she devoted her life to doing nice things for people. Most of what she accomplished was geared toward empowering the less fortunate, and she didn't have much herself. To this day, I'm stunned by my mother's empathy and humanity for people from all walks of life. My mother had a special place in her heart for pregnant teens. She knew it would be a long road ahead of them. Many times, that road was traveled alone – mentally, physically, financially, and emotionally.

To my dismay, godparents are an endangered species these days. Fortunately, I was blessed with Mrs. Gertie Graham, who supported my mother and me for my entire life—a true godmother. Mrs. Graham is the epitome of a heaven-sent angel—a prototype godmother if you will. The things she's done for me make me emotional to this day, so much so that every keystroke of this keyboard is like her heartbeat. I can even feel the presence of my mother's hand resting on my recently surgically-repaired shoulder. The death of my mother made Mrs. Graham's role in my life even more vital. Furthermore, I had to come to terms with taking Mrs. Graham for granted over the years. Godparents are real, and more good people like them are needed.

Certain teachers, like Mrs. Hill from School #65 in Buffalo, NY, were nice to me. Mrs. Gabala and Ms. Williams from Lewis J. Bennett High School in Buffalo, NY were brutally honest with me but nice in their approach. Both educators were gracious, and their classrooms felt like safe places to learn and grow. Mrs. Gabala knew I was scared of math but reinforced the need to master the subject to be successful in life, even after I dropped her class.

Growing up, in the Town Boys and Girls Club in the Black Rock-Riverside community of Buffalo, NY, I was surrounded by kind people. The kindest of them all was the one and only Bob "Kat" Nowack. "Bob," as he was affectionately known, was a father figure to me and many youth in the Shaffer Village Housing projects, aka "The Proj". Bob, a middle-aged white man with kids of his own, gave 120 percent of himself to thousands of kids who looked nothing like him. Once, someone asked him, "What could I do to repay you"? He responded, "Give back when you are in a position to give back. Give time and money, but importantly give time."

My best friends, Lamont and Kanika Cunninham, are simply kind people in many ways. They raised the standard and upheld a standard that I try to emulate. As a single dad raising a daughter, having a law enforcement career, and being on-call for work for eleven years, they were vital to raising Sadaija. Kanika, is a second mom, and Lamont is the father figure in my absence. During a difficult time between my ex-wife and me, my police academy date was set to start. My girlfriend at the time, T.R.W., helped care for Sadaija. Again, she was the epitome of kindness.

The irony of being kind and giving back abundantly is rewarding. It makes you feel good inside; it humanizes you in a way that can't be purchased.

No drug or alcoholic beverage can equate to the high you receive. Random acts of kindness are also beautiful gestures. Simply being kind and doing something nice for someone that cannot do anything for you is the ultimate flex.

VIBE

Tupac – "**Smile**"
Daryl Hall & John Oates – "**Sara Smile**"

About my dear friend, affectionately known as “Coach Chestnut”:

He is more than just a coach. He is so down to earth, brilliant, talented, and multifaceted in areas that one could only imagine. He is in no way a typical guy. I have had the pleasure of slowly getting to know him while working as a colleague for over eight years. Why slowly? Well, I have to feel people out, check and double check their vibe . . . He is so observant, too . . . so I had to observe the observer . . . . Get my drift? So, while delving into this book, imagine a hood dude, but with the likeness and talents of Bezos . . . ! Just “hooder,” calm, cool, and all the way collected, too! It has been my pleasure getting to know my friend, not only as an educator but as a true battle buddy and a loving, giving father, my ride or die. He’s a down dude, a dying breed.

So, while you’re reading his story, know this: he keeps it “100” all the time. He is a living testimony that anyone can make it out, and under any circumstances. And lastly, this guy is as sweet as pie, but don’t test him because you will see the waters are muddy.

DaDawn Taylor
Educator

SAVE SOME MONEY

Making money, growing money, and entrepreneurial opportunities are all important but impossible without saving some of your own money.

Saving money is a key to stability and reducing stress. Having my own money on hand has been one of the single most stress-reducing power moves I've made. It has allowed me to take advantage of exclusive investment opportunities. For example, a particular land investment cost me nine thousand dollars cash. In less than two years, it quadrupled in value. I'm not rich, but I have been able to keep enough money on hand to keep trials and tribulations from engulfing me into total financial hardship. Most of my friends make more money than I do, but I've been able to have some of the same things they have. Also, when it's time to travel, go out to dinner, attend concerts and comedy shows, and socialize comfortably, I can pay my way. I've never been the one to be a financial burden to anyone, especially my parents and close friends. Furthermore, it feels good to have your own. Some say money is the root of all evil. I say the lack of financial freedom will cause you to do ugly things, and over time, you may become evil. I have dated and had relationships for the wrong reasons because, at times, my finances were trash.

VIBE

Jay-Z – "**4:44**"
Cardi B – "**Money**"

INVEST

Many times, when people see the word "invest," instantaneously the stock market or real estate comes to mind. However, my conversation is about investing in oneself and our youth. Invest in your name and skill set. Cultivate your intellectual property before running out and just getting a job. Ask yourself, "Can I make money from something that I am passionate about or something I'm simply good at doing?" Identify your talents and the talents of people in your circle. You just may discover you're already a business. Build the business, brand the name, scale your brand and business, and promote your brand.

I took my gift of gab and my hustler's mentality in 1998 and purchased my first duplex for $30,000 in Buffalo, NY at age twenty-five. At the time, I was in an unhealthy marriage to which I contributed to the toxicity and had the responsibility of raising a four-year-old daughter. I knew the house itself wasn't an ideal "home," but the return of the rents from each unit supported the lifestyle I wanted but could not afford.

My R.O.I. (return on investment) was competitive.

This type of investment is vital when looking toward your future – ten and fifteen years from now, not just three to five years. **You must set the standard for your children and those you lead by providing visible examples.** This same vision forced me to change the way I raised/managed my children. My son, Maceo, will reap the benefits of this philosophy the most because he doesn't know a different way to do things. My daughter, Sadaija, and I grew simultaneously in this direction while I was raising her. Foolishly I had a "watch me and take notes" perspective and transitioned to "what do you think about this idea?" The bottom line: investing in yourself and our youth will keep our community and economy vibrant.

VIBE

Jay-Z, Beanie Segal, Scarface, Jadakiss – **"Somehow Some Way"**

CHANGE IS A CHALLENGE

Change is going to happen whether you want it to or not. Embrace it.

Change is consistent. Change is inevitable.

The good thing about change is it helps you grow and shift to levels you never knew you had. Change is fun, painful, and referenceable, even if it's to the extent of a relationship ending or a new one ascending, or moving to a new neighborhood. In with the new, out with the old. Change exposes you to yourself! Change demands you to ask yourself: "What am I made of? Who am I? When am I going to act? Will I bet on myself?"

Change keeps you alive.

Change provides you with tangible reference points where you can see your growth. Embracing change is growth.

In a six-year period, I've purchased five properties, sold two, and netted six figures from my willingness to accept and embrace change.

VIBE

Anthony Hamilton – **"Point of It All"**
Leela James – **"All Over Again"**

THE DOG IN YOU

What's its purpose? Where does it derive from? The development of that "dog" in you, also known as the "GO TIME" in you . . . it's that thing that gives you the ability to do the things that people say you can't do. The sense of urgency to do the things you think you're too tired to do. That "dog" in you develops when you go beyond what you believe you can accomplish. Fire and desire are the heart and soul of that dog within you. It is that emotional voice that tells you, "The time is now . . . dominate, overcome, finish."

My fire and desire have kept me awake countless nights with dreams, thoughts, and ideas that I cannot explain. All I know is that it has purpose because it has taken me to heights I didn't know I could achieve.

Be sure to tap into that "DOG" in you anytime you see fit.

VIBE

Wale & SZA – **"The Need to Know"**
Rick James – **"Fire & Desire"**

ZIP CODES AND AREA CODES

Where you're from does not dictate where you're going. Your zip code has nothing to do with where you're trying to go or what you're meant to do. Don't let where you come from stop you, your destiny, your drive, or the essence of what makes you, you. It does not matter if you're from a small town or a big city.

Whenever I needed to travel home, I had to prepare myself mentally. I got butterflies, and my nerves went into a frenzy. I had several panic attacks before and during my 1,500-mile round trip trek from Tennessee to Buffalo. For years, I've kept this a secret from everyone except my son's mother and my confidant, Mumumba. Several people from Buffalo who've left our hometown have described the same feeling as though it were a dark cloud over our city because of the lack of growth in many areas, which is evident on the east side of the city. The residents have been tolerant for decades while awaiting change. Regardless, I believe that the city of Buffalo has prepared me for everything that I've been experiencing throughout my life. I'm battle tested. My zip code does not dictate my success, but it has prepared me for success. Don't let anyone tell you just because you're from a certain location, city, town, or neighborhood that you aren't "the one." You can do or be anything you set your mind to.

LEAD OR BE LED!

VIBE

Anthony Hamilton – **"Comin' From Where I'm From"**
Kanye West – **"Homecoming"**

GIRL POWER

A female must have multiple options to dictate and control her trajectory. After raising a daughter and coaching girls for twenty-one years, I quickly learned that the key to success for most females is having options. Options allow females to make decisions that males can't dictate or prepare for. Options empower females to seek healthy, meaningful situations where they can grow. Options deter females from becoming stagnant or having a sense of entitlement. A sense of "girl power" is a must; females must have options. Females cannot afford to get boxed in. Being mentally, physically, and emotionally aware is a necessity. Many men crumble when they see the emotions of women, then tend to be untruthful about what they really want or how they really feel. In order for females to obtain the truth within a man, women need to manage their emotions properly. That is the key to getting to the bottom of things.

VIBE

Etta James – **"I'd Rather Go Blind"**
Destiny's Child – **"Survivor"**

Dear Reader,

Everything in life happens for a reason, and for one reason or another, you have been called to this book. But this is no ordinary book; it's a journey. The journey of a man who found success in a world where many would have failed. His journey is one of truth, inspiration, and boldness and demands attention as you read through the powerful notes.

Some may ask, "Why Coach Chestnut? What is so special about his story?" Coach Chestnut is not a superstar or a name known all over the country. He's a regular person like you or me, and it's exactly why you should dive into his journey. He talks about struggles that many of us have faced but may be uncomfortable discussing with others. He doesn't shy away from the trials that made him the man he is today. By embracing his faults and lessons learned, he gives us all a space to be authentic and proud of our own journeys. We don't need another story about a famous person. We need to hear from people that have lived through our struggles and come out on the other end even stronger.

I met this man while working together at a high school and could immediately see that he was different. He wasn't someone who always knew he wanted to teach, but he knew he was called to it. And he followed his heart. He wasn't perfect, and many doubted some of his techniques with students, but he stayed true to who he was. It created an environment where others felt safe enough to be seen and heard. He had the unique ability to reach those that many thought were lost or on the wrong path, and he made it his mission to never leave them hanging. It wasn't easy, but he showed up every day for his students like they were family. It's why he's beloved by those that have crossed paths with him.

I challenge you to take a step back and soak in the powerful notes shared throughout this book. You may not relate to all of them, but you will find a piece of you somewhere throughout this journey. We need more stories about *us*, about the regular people who get up and make things happen every day. How can we inspire each other? By sharing our survival stories with others and inspiring others to do the same. Open your mind and enjoy the ride.

Dr. Chiquita S. Jackson
Educator/Counselor

KARMA IS CONTAGIOUS

Embrace your karma. You are not innocent.

Ladies and gentlemen, boys and girls, friends and foes . . . this is self-reflection at its best.

Believe this: how you treat others will come back to you. When that time comes, you must embrace it. It will come. You must embrace it. Don't get mad. Don't get frustrated. Understand the same thing that you've done to somebody will be done to you. So, when it comes, it's your job to embrace it. You've not loved. You've not done the right thing. You've cheated. You've not given your all. You have not embraced things and/or people authentically. You have not been the best person that you can be. You have made mistakes. You have let goals go. You have underestimated people, and you have let people down. "People" have done the same thing to you. When it comes to karma, embrace it and be humbled by it. Accept it. I was once told by someone I cared for very much that the worst thing I ever did to her was "withhold love." She could accept everything else, but to withhold love was worse than being cheated on. As the "Urban Survivor," I felt that from the moment the statement left her lips.

Karma will not let you off the hook. Karma will not skip you. Karma collects all debts, even if your children have to pay them.

VIBE

Tyrese – **"Shame"**
Tank – **"I Deserve"**
Tupac feat. Michel'le – **"Run Tha Streetz"**
Leela James – **"Fall for You"**
Eminem feat. Rihanna – **"Love the Way You Lie"**

PASSION MAY BE YOUR PURPOSE

Passion, many times, is your purpose. It is the "why" for what you do. When you know why, you understand why you're up late. You understand why you've walked six miles to get to your destination. Passion provides the reason for signing up for that marathon or the cross-country team. Some high school students sign up for sports to avoid having to babysit younger siblings or to reduce interactions with their parents. True passions will have you put yourself on punishment. Passion asks you to be your own cheerleader. Make sure you properly identify your passion and always maintain your purpose.

My passion is EMPOWERING YOUTH.

VIBE

Michel'le – **"Something in My Heart"**
Lenny Williams – **"'Cause I Love You"**
Gerald Levert – **"Baby Hold on to Me"**

PURPOSE DICTATES YOUR INTENTION

Purpose is essentially your intention and reasoning of your "why." Many times, your purpose comes from within. It's emotional and sometimes kept to yourself because of its fragility. Your enemies will always go after your purpose to stop your progress. Protect your purpose at all costs. Developing as an individual and as a brand has many facets. My purpose has always been to uplift my family and, specifically, raise the bar for my children, nieces, and nephews. From the age of eight years old, I've felt it was meant for me to push my family, the vision, and expectations forward. As my coaching career took shape, I felt it was also my purpose to take student-athletes that could not see their own potential to the next level. Over the years, I quickly gained the ability to identify talent immediately. Then, I strategically invested in people to cultivate that talent (most times free of charge).

VIBE

Jay-Z – **"Young Forever"**
Eric B & Rakim – **"Microphone Fiend"**
LL Cool J – **"I'm Bad"**

GOALS

Everyone must have goals. Goals should be documented, fluid, attainable, and celebrated when accomplished. What do you want to accomplish next month? What do you want to accomplish next year? Where do you see yourself two years from now? What do you want five years from now? You must have goals. Goals help you map out your plan, avenue of approach, and logistical obstacles. Goals are essential. Goals should have a suspense date. Goals are needed. Be goal oriented. Set your realistic goals and design a custom plan of action.

Most importantly, review your goals and celebrate them.

VIBE

Tupac – **"Picture Me Rollin'"**
50 Cent – **"In Da Club"**

CHALLENGES OF A STROLLER

You need challenges just to evolve. Every month you should try to have a new challenge for a minimum of 21 days. It can be simple, such as getting up an extra 30 minutes earlier, doing 21 push-ups a day, no meat, no dairy. Find something that you consistently have to do that you typically would not do. On one occasion, I signed up for the Beltline 10K race in Atlanta. I was aware that I was not good enough to win the race, but I selected several people during the race that no matter what, I was going to beat them. In all accounts, I applied pressure to myself and to achieve a greater outcome.

Furthermore, I learned to not underestimate the women running with a three-wheeled stroller with a toddler on board. They are pretty darn strong and resilient.

VIBE

Tupac – **"Against All Odds"**
Jay-Z – **"What More Can I Say"**
Tupac – **"Changes"**
Eminem – **"The Way I Am"**

MOTO THE MIND

Motivational influences should be consumed daily because they have a short shelf life.

Motivation is a temporary spark that fuels your adrenaline. As a track coach, I always wanted to motivate my runners to reach their potential. My goal was to push them beyond their known abilities. I always positioned myself at the corner of the last 110 meters of the track or the last 600 meters of a cross-country meet and demanded more. I would say, "NOW . . . NOW . . . HEAD DOWN, NOW," then I would witness a shift and an acceleration—another gear not seen in practice. I wanted more because I knew what I'd invested in each and every one of them. No stopwatch needed. I just demanded, "More . . . give me more," and I reminded them, "You're stronger than your opponents."

Salute to all my track and cross-country family from Bennett High School, student-athletes from Hershey Track Clarksville, the Clarksville All-Stars, and West Creek High School Track & Cross-Country teams-Clarksville, TN.

However, the caveat to motivation is commitment!

If you only excel when you are motivated, then you're not committed. You must use motivation as your vehicle toward commitment. Commitment promotes consistency. Consistency will separate you from your peers and position you to compete against the greats. Competing against the greats puts you in position to be the GOAT (greatest of all time), then people crown the GOATS. There are levels to motivation, commitment, and consistency; the ability needed to succeed lies in each and every one of us.

LEAD OR BE LED.

VIBE

T.I. – **"Motivation"**
Moneybagg Yo – **"Me vs. Me"**

PERCEPTIONS X 2

The thing about perception is that two people can witness, read, and experience the same tragic event and have completely different outcomes. At one point in my life, I wanted to own a million dollars' worth of property and drive a respectable car. Then, my queen, Shirley Webb-Hall, and my Road Dog, Clyde J. Chestnut, passed away, and I found myself parentless. I was like an explorer without a map and a hole in his heart. I was speechless about my mother's death but expressive of my father's. It was weird to me. This spun me into a level of depression I could not mask. I felt emotionally empty, which my children, students, and athletes I coached observed. Suddenly, my passion for life had been compromised. Not only did I have to acknowledge my emotions, but had to deal with my siblings' emotions, too. Some of my close friends had also lost their parents. My new perception has me focusing on a million-dollar mindset and a billion dollars' worth of memories and experiences.

VIBE

Jay-Z feat. Gloria Carter – **"Smile"**
Jay-Z – **"Legacy"**
Terrence Howard (*Hustle & Flow*) – **"It's Hard Out Here for a Pimp"**

LIVE FEARLESSLY

To go after your future, you gotta live fearlessly. This was the mantra I placed at the feet of my daughter as she left for basic training in the United States Marines. However, before her departure, I asked her what her backup plan was if she didn't make it. Right in that moment of silence, I knew I had violated everything I preached. But DNA will always provide clarification every time. Sadaija (or "Daija Doo" as I call her) responded, "I have no back-up plan. I'm going to be a United States Marine." From that point, we've been living fearlessly . . . In true DNA fashion, my son, without any preparation, has taken the baton and lived fearlessly since his exit from the womb.

VIBE

Nipsey Hussle feat. Belly & Dom Kennedy – **"Double Up"**
Jay-Z feat. Blue Ivy – **"Glory"**
2 Chainz feat. Kevin Gates – **"I Feel Like"**

LEADERS LEAD FROM THE FRONT, NOT THE REAR

When you're a leader you must practice what you preach. When you're the leader you must abstain from crying and complaining to those you lead. Furthermore, those that you're leading don't care anyway, that's what you get paid the big bucks for. When in charge, take charge . . . LEAD OR BE LED!

Being a leader is a privilege for the few that have the ability to maintain the standard and reinforce the standard of those that they are responsible for. As a leader, you must take care of your people, and in time they will learn to take care of you. Keep in mind, it takes time for those you are responsible for to buy into whatever you're promoting. Growth and trust are ongoing, and you must earn the respect of those you care for, and reinforce that respect periodically.

VIBE

Commodores – **"Easy"**
Aloe Blacc – **"The Man"**

LOVE

Love is nothing more than a misunderstanding between two fools . . . But you got to be willing to be a little foolish to fall in love. This is an area where conventional wisdom goes right out the door by everyone, says everyone! Real relationships take work, kindness, sacrifice, teamwork, understanding, empathy, and emotional investment. You will disappoint someone, and someone will disappoint you. At some point, you will be hurt, and you will hurt someone. However, physical or emotional abuse are unacceptable and cannot be given a pass. Just because it looks good or bad on paper does not mean it's reality. People who want the most successful relationships will be forced to commit time and effort to reach the real essence of a person. Make no mistake about it, this is an investment. Invest wisely and enthusiastically! Pay attention to your gut instinct. Don't ignore facts. Actions will always speak louder than words. Understand that just because someone loves you or you've got love for someone does not mean you'll spend the rest of your life with that person.

Throughout your life, you could possibly have several loves. The act of love and the process of love is intoxicating.

In the end, if it's right, love will win. LOVE WINS EVERY TIME.

VIBE

Keyshia Cole – **"Love"**
Keyshia Cole – **"I Should Have Cheated"**

Jaheim feat. Keyshia Cole – **"I've Changed"**
Usher – **"U Got It Bad"**
Usher – **"Papers"**
Usher – **"Moving Mountains"**

To Generation Z:

This book, at its core, is not just a book. It's a manual of sorts. If you've ever heard the saying, "bought sense is better than given sense," consider this given sense gathered through the writer's years of bought sense. This is a piece that's full of practical information. The kind of information that prepares you for life, careers, and relationships, especially after weighty life changes. This book is an important resource, written in a way that can be understood and connected with. Each chapter inspires and teaches how to build the foundation for your "brand" through having intentional confidence. It also teaches how to protect that brand by protecting yourself via venting and communicating your emotions. It instructs how to grow your "brand" by growing your mind and educating yourself. It inspires you to conquer stereotypes by using the things society says are obstacles as your personal stepping-stones to the goals you want to achieve. It encourages self-reflection and taking responsibility for the seeds you sow in the world and the harvest you reap. It instructs how to depend on yourself, instead of the relationships you may find yourself in. If you are a self-starter and on the road to entrepreneurship, introducing yourself to these concepts is the perfect starting point.

Lyric T. Brooks
Former Student

REALITY COMES AT YOU FAST

When you take time to plan out a specific plan of action, reality comes fast. Your who, what, when, where, why, and how will demand a reaction or response expeditiously. There's an old saying: "Be careful what you wish for; you just might get it."

You must stay ready so that you don't have to get ready. Understand that what you wish for and dream of many times comes when you're least prepared for it.

VIBE

Drake - **"0 to 100/The Catch Up"**

CONFIDENCE IS NO COINCIDENCE

At age eight, I started riding the city bus to summer camp. By age nine, I was smoking my father's and siblings' cigarette butts from the ashtray. At ten years old, I had my first pistol. By age twelve, I had my first sexual experience, experimented with marijuana, stole several BMX bicycles and sold them for profit, and had my first job making $5 an hour working at the Town Boys & Girls Club. Before my fifteenth birthday, I got my first win against a grown man in a physical altercation and had already started learning how to drive. By sixteen, I had a driver's license, bank account, and jobs at Burger King and Hamlin Terrace Nursing Home. I was peddling nickel bags of marijuana and selling boosted women's clothing out of my high school locker. I bought my first car (1981 Buick Skylark) and sold Burger King products in the projects to pay for my car insurance, which was $100 a month.

At home, money had gotten tight for my mother, so I assumed financial responsibility for the phone and cable bills. At seventeen, I had regular access to one of the most popular luxury cars in the hood, the infamous Acura Legend. My popularity as a dominant high school athlete came full circle. My dating pool expanded dramatically, so I found myself more interested in females who had money and were enrolled in college. My best friend, Lamont, was as solid as they came and is still loyal to this day. Also, I had a couple of different circles I ran with. My fellow athletes' squad, my "get it how we live" squad, my friends from the "projects," and my "suburban friends," along with my Italian girlfriend, K.V., whom I had to keep a secret due to dynamics similar to the movie *A Bronx Tale* (1993). I joined the military, became a law enforcement officer, worked child sex abuse cases and homicide cases, was a crisis negotiator, undercover operator, and mobile device forensics examinator, and became an educator and a track coach. All had a purpose. My confidence is no coincidence!

I am a firm believer that youth need to be mentored with confidence from positive influences. I've confirmed with several mental health professionals who agree: Supreme confidence is one of the best tools to reduce teen suicide.

VIBE

Kanye West – **"Bound 2"**
Jay-Z & Kanye West – **"Ni**as in Paris"**

VALUE

Seek to value yourself or you will depreciate. Simply put, surround yourself with people that will help you grow and expand. Your circle should have the liberty to ask you the hard questions and facilitate uncomfortable conversations. If you hang around nine broke friends, you're bound to be the tenth.

Find your tribe wherever you are present. This could be at work, school, or church. It's okay to have multiple tribes.

VIBE

Gary Portnoy & Judy Hart-Angelo – ***Cheers*** **theme song**
Whodini – **"Friends"**
Kanye West feat. Jamie Foxx – **"Gold Digger"**

VIBES AND ENERGY

When an organic or invested person is in your presence, they can feel everything. Vibes and energy are real things. The transfer of vibes and energy from one person to another is an amazing experience, and I hope at some point everyone will experience it. If you have the gift of "presence" or the ability to change the temperature of a room by your mere presence, that's a gift and a curse. Embrace both extremes. But understand that most won't understand it or accept it. They may even misinterpret it.

VIBE

Whodini - Five Minutes of Funk Afrika Bambaataa & SoulSonic Force – **"Planet Rock"**
Soho – **"Hot Music"**

BE RESOURCEFUL. DON'T GIVE UP.

If you have a smartphone, do smart things on your smartphone. Before you try to conquer the whole world by yourself, check your circle of friends. What skills do your friends have that you may be able to utilize? As a citizen, I have seen things that I believe should be addressed and corrected, so I sought the office of a city councilman to make a change. I worked hard, but I tried to do it all on my own. Although I did have some help and obtained 35% of the vote, I didn't have a team. I did not properly utilize my resources.

VIBE

Rob Base & DJ EZ Rock – **"It Takes Two"**
Chill/Spadley feat. Detective Chestnut – **"Oh Why"**

LOVE SOUNDS LIKE AND LOOKS LIKE LOVE

When your love for someone is solid, you won't seek validation. You will care less about "what-ifs" and more about "what's next." You will jump out of a perfectly good plane, take on white water rapids, and fly across the globe, feeling unbothered by the day or month while happily being present. A caretaker of another's smile and heart . . . that's love.

VIBE

Rob Base & DJ EZ Rock – **"Joy and Pain"**
Cardi B – **"Be Careful"**
Lil' Kim – **"Hold On"**
Leela James – **"Fall for You"**
Floetry – **"Say Yes"**
Maxwell – **"Pretty Wings"**
The Black Eyed Peas – **"Where Is the Love?"**
Wale feat. Usher – **"Matrimony"**
Keith Sweat – **"I'll Give All My Love to You"**
Wyclef Jean feat. Mary J. Blige – **"911"**
Kem – **"Love Calls"**

WHEN IN DOUBT

When in doubt, be still for a moment.

Then ask yourself who, what, when, where, why, how.

Keep your plan of approach simple but detailed, direct, and specific. Then execute!

VIBE

George Tandy Jr. – **"March"**
Bobby Brown – **"My Prerogative"**

JUST BECAUSE YOU MADE IT DOES NOT MEAN YOU'RE DONE

Even after you've "made it," you must set the standard, raise the standard, or uphold the standard. Then, prepare those that will come after you to carry on the standard. The process of passing the baton, whether it's in a sport or life, is a real thing. Just because you become a millionaire or reach your designated goal doesn't mean your work is done. It's not over. The key is to reinvest the million dollars so that you can make another million dollars. Just because you finally got the person you want doesn't mean your work is done. It's not over. You must then transition to cultivating the relationship.

VIBE

Marvin Sapp – **"Never Would Have Made It"**
Busta Rhymes feat. Linkin Park – **"We Made It"**

FEELINGS

Your feelings are a form of emotions; emotions can cloud facts. Facts can stand on their own.

When conducting business, stay fact-based, focused, cognizant of your feelings, and read the room.

When you decide to purchase something expensive and have to negotiate the price and terms, your feelings will get involved. Remind yourself: it's just business.

VIBE

Jay-Z feat. Alicia Keys – **"Empire State of Mind"**
Kevin Gates – **"Power"**
Kevin Gates – **"In My Feelings"**

MOTIVATION IS TEMPORARY

Motivational words from the likes of TD Jakes, Eric Thomas, and Les Brown will need to be replenished regularly, if not daily. Therefore, you must reinforce it with purpose and commitment to the vision of a finished product. The good part is that you typically hear something new every time you review the same media.

VIBE

Alicia Keys – **"If I Ain't Got You"**
Big Daddy Kane – **"I Get the Job Done"**
Big Daddy Kane – **"Ain't No Half-Steppin'"**

LOYALTY IS LIMITED

Anything or anyone left unattended or not maintained will go bad.

This goes for being in a relationship, owning a pet, and even having a car. You cannot allow a car to sit for weeks and months at a time and expect it to perform at its best when it's time to travel. A car needs to be driven; fluids, gasses, and air must flow through tubes and hoses. Spark plugs need to be activated, tires need to roll, lights need to shine, and horns need to make noise. This should also be applied to friendships and relationships. If you do not stay engaged and active, they, too, will erode, right along with their loyalty.

VIBE

Kendrick Lamar feat. Rihanna – **"Loyalty"**
Drake feat. Rihanna – **"Take Care"**
SZA – **"The Weekend"**

INTUITION MUST BE TESTED BEFORE IT CAN BE TRUSTED

At some point, you must test the little voice that speaks to you from within. The voice that gets its information from your intuition that we all ignore. Well not me . . . anymore. My intuition has been tested. I've taken those chances and overall, I'm accepting of my results. However, your intuitions must be tested several times to validate them. Intuitions must be tested in various situations involving a variety of people. Your experiences, knowledge, reasonings, and travels have a great impact on your intuitions.

Travel and exposure to different environments and culture is vital in honing this skill set.

VIBE

Ella Mai – **"Boo'd Up"**
Ella Mai – **"Trip"**
Wale feat. Rihanna – **"Bad"**
Chill w/ Armored Sound Productions – **"Paid Dues"**
Nat King Cole – **"That's All"**

CLICHÉS

Clichés, at one time, were good advice, but they have been taken for granted. Don't let good advice go to waste; take what applies and store the rest away. Everyone is guilty of stealing and sharing memes and catechisms, then sharing them on our favorite social media platforms. However, prior to memes, the information was once good advice that was ignored.

VIBE

Ed Sheeran – **"Thinking Out Loud"**
Bruno Mars – **"Grenade"**
Lauryn Hill – **"Nothing Even Matters"**

TRAVEL

For your own personal growth, you must travel! Leave your area code multiple times, or relocate so that you can grow in unimaginable ways. The relocation doesn't have to be permanent, but it is a getaway for a new set of experiences and expectations.

Without a doubt, one of my biggest power moves was joining the United States Army, which took me out of my comfort zone. I graduated from high school and was enrolled at Buffalo State College, but I had already gotten off track. During the summer after my high school graduation, I was drinking, smoking, partying, fornicating, and committing unnecessary petty crimes. I was definitely lost and unsure of how I got into this space. I believe I had a sense of "I made it" and became unmotivated and unfocused. Furthermore, once all my friends and associates began preparing to go away for college, I felt like an underachiever. Right then, I knew I should have taken the football scholarship I was offered at a school three hours away. Arrogantly, I thought I was too good for the school.

Enlisting in the military gave me the travel and the money I was missing. For me, hopping in the car and cranking out a 1,500-mile round trip was nothing. Travel allows you to grow spiritually and emotionally; it forms several levels of patience. Travel teaches you to pay attention to your surroundings and learn how to read a room. When you travel to Europe, Asia, and South America, your safety is key. Having a good time is secondary. Travel forces you to culturally expose yourself and respect the cultures of others. Travel teaches you that there are different ways to accomplish many things. When you travel, you quickly learn the influence of music and how its strength connects all races and genders.

Traveling is amazing.

VIBE

Adele – **"Someone Like You"**
Tupac – **"Can U Get Away"**
Eminem – **"Lose Yourself"**

SUICIDE

Suicide is not an option. Suicide is not a solution. People love you.

As a new homicide investigator, I had the impression that I would be out chasing serial killers, participating in statewide manhunts, saving families from burning houses set by arsonists, and engaging in late-night shootouts. Some of that did happen, but as a homicide investigator, you will also find yourself responding to all unattended deaths, including suicides. My first suicide was that of a ten-year-old boy that looked like me when I was his age. In his suicide note, he mentioned being bullied because of his dark complexion. This, too, was all too familiar in my life. I was so dark that I was called "Mobil oil," "tar baby," "Manute Bol's son," "Chocolate Thunder," "dookie boy," and "Kunta Kinte." I could go on and on. I was made to believe I was ugly and unfit for society. My DNA provided me with a barrel chest, thick neck, shoulders like Mount Rushmore, quads like a young stallion, and tight skin like high-end leather and durable as Teflon. I've only used sunscreen a handful of times in my life. Why bother with my infinite wisdom? Looking in a mirror and taking pictures is something I avoided all through my childhood. As an adult, I have to remind folks to cut the flash on when taking a picture of me. Everyone laughs, but I am dead serious. As a kid, I recall once looking in the mirror and saying, "Damn you're black." I temporarily believed the opinions of others.

But then my dad spoke. One conversation changed my whole world. My dad asked, "Do any of these people who are talking about you . . . love you? Care about you? Feed you? Help you? Stick up for you?" Of course, my answer was "no." My dad said, "BOY, F*** THEM PEOPLE!" **I felt that**!

But it wasn't the curse word that freed me. It was one of many experiences called the transfer of energy. The energy coming from my dad was all I needed. He continued to tell me how, from that day forward, I was to make sure I walked with my chin held up, chest out, and shoulders pinned back. When speaking, I was to project my voice. At the time, I was about ten years old, and he didn't know I was already in possession of my first pistol. My dad also reminded me that I had the right to protect myself at all times. However, I was forbidden to put my hands on anyone first. But if someone put their hands on me, I better beat that a** and beat their a** so good they would not be interested in ever fighting me again. My dad was clear when he said, "You need to be one and done." This conversation gave me all the confidence about myself that I needed at the time. More importantly, my family and friends always instilled confidence in me.

Somehow, we must find a way to instill that same confidence in our youth. Our youth need to be held accountable and empowered simultaneously. Mental health professionals confirmed my belief that *confidence* is an important factor in reducing suicide. I've previously stated that "confidence is no coincidence." Be deliberate in reinforcing confidence. This is the key to reducing teen suicide and opening the lines of communication. When a person contemplates taking their life, they will cry out for help. They will show signs. They will make statements. This is our cue, as a society, to act because you rarely get multiple chances to do so. With that being said, once a person has decided to take their own life, there's little anyone can do.

VIBE

Bruno Mars – **"Just the Way You Are"**
Miley Cyrus – **"Wrecking Ball"**
Whitney Houston – **"I Have Nothing"**
Whitney Houston – **"I Will Always Love You"**
T.I. feat. Rihanna – **"Live Your Life"**

FRIEND

Sometimes you gotta be that one friend. At some point, you may need to be that friend that changes the dynamics of your group of friends. You've got to push the pack forward. This could be in business, travel, expectations, and/or vision. A friendship is all about give and take, just like any other relationship. It's an investment in another person and advantageous to your growth to allow or to be allowed to have a front row seat to another human's triumphs, trials, and tribulations. Friendships also take time to develop but can be ruined in no time at all; loyalty must be reciprocated.

VIBE

Too Short – **"Blow the Whistle"**
Jay-Z – **"Do U Wanna Ride"**

PARENTS

Parenting does not end at eighteen years of age. Parents owe it to their children to provide options and opportunities. Luxury brand cars, shoes, bags, and toys are not options but amenities. Preparation to be self-sufficient is the goal. In return, children need to be coachable and teachable. They should provide their parents feedback and show visible growth. Essentially, once a child has graduated from high school, a parent should be able to transition into the management phase of parenting. There are specific responsibilities children should take on without question. As the growth continues, the next shift will allow the parent to become a type of mentor. In this space and time, I believe a parent and child will see the most growth in their relationship. Be open to change.

VIBE

Whitney Houston – **"I Look to You"**
Luther Vandross – **"Dance with My Father"**

BE WITH PEOPLE ENTHUSIASTICALLY

Unfortunately, everyone I know, including myself, has found themselves being somewhere with someone they didn't want to be with. This is where you learn to say, "No thank you" or "Thanks for the offer." Strive to be in the presence of those who cultivate good energy, not those who drain your energy. Learn to detach from negative people as soon as possible. Learning this skill is not as easy as it may seem because most people hate to hurt the feelings of another. The phrase "keeping it 100%" can cause some extensive pain. Most of us are really keeping it 85% just to reduce verbal and physical confrontations.

VIBE

Michael Jackson – **"Man in the Mirror"**
Dru Hill – **"We're Not Making Love No More"**
Tony Toni Tone – **"Just Me and You"**
Mystikal – **"Here I Go"**
Meek Mill – **"Expensive Pain"**

So many words flow effortlessly as I think about the ones that best describe DeMone Chestnut.

Where do I even begin? For starters, the obvious: educator, former detective, coach, father, son, friend, and veteran. For those who know him on a deeper level: loyal, lifelong learner, doer, advocate, and empowerer. He has the keen ability and GIFT to identify strengths in others and help them see it in themselves. Leader. Positive vibes. Go-getter. Real. Raw. Powerful. Entrepreneurial spirit. Encourager. Risk-taker. Highly motivated. Lover of music. Funny. Hustler. Intelligent. Deep thinker. Insightful. Impactful. Genuine. Adventurous. Energy. Demands respect. Risk taker. Blunt, but has couth. Life speaker. Street smart. Savvy. GREATNESS. This book will be nothing short of all this combined and rolled up into one.

I first met DeMone Chestnut when I was working as a substitute teacher at the same high school as him. He put in a good word for me and helped me get the job as the assistant track coach. Being young and fresh out of college, I lacked experience, so when I applied for an open teacher position, self-doubt crept in. I will never forget a life-changing conversation we had while walking across the track field one day during practice. He asked how the job interview went, and I downplayed it and said I probably would not get the job. He stopped me on the spot and said, "Don't do that. Don't talk down about yourself, even jokingly. Speak that shit into existence and claim it." These types of wisdom nuggets are the types of impactful lessons you can expect to learn from the *Survival Guide*. I had the pleasure of working alongside him for years and learned so much about coaching, teaching, and life from him. Some of the most impactful lessons I learned from him were about loyalty (to this day, he has my back), teamwork, and speaking life into myself and others. His friendship has helped shape me into who I am today. I am greater because I know him and have been influenced by him. I'm not the only person who can say that he has changed their life for the better. The Survival Guide will provide the reader with a front row seat to the knowledge he has to share. DeMone turns all his talents and gifts into a hustle. The fact that he will now be a published author is right on brand for him. He's collected all his wisdom and is turning it into a survival guide to share the knowledge he's learned throughout his life. What he has to say transcends all ages, all races and ethnicities, and all walks of life. If you want to level up in life, become a more fearless leader, and improve your mindset, then read and apply the survival tips that Coach Chestnut has to say.

Lori Taylor
Educator

KNOW YOUR RIGHTS

As an American citizen, you must know your fundamental rights, especially your Bill of Rights. There's no need to be a scholar in that area, but you should know enough to understand right from wrong. When things are done wrong, file an official record of the complaint and aggressively follow up with it. Please understand, if it's not documented on paper, it does not exist and never happened. This includes when you are dealing with the law, your employment, the school system, the government, a business, and contracts.

VIBE

Public Enemy – **"Fight the Power"**
Public Enemy – **"Black Steel in the Hour of Chaos"**

DECISIONS

As a leader, one of the most important aspects of your authority will be making sound decisions. While managing your personal life, tough decisions will need to be made. Get comfortable making decisions. You should make sound decisions based on facts, training, and circumstances, not emotions. There is no "one size fits all." Be willing to accept advice, but make sure the final decision is yours and stand ten toes down on your decision. When you make a mistake, own it. Make peace with your strengths and weaknesses because you will not be able to hide them. Know that your training, knowledge, skill set, and natural instinct will be your voice of reason on many occasions. As a leader, it's OK to not know everything or have the answer to every question. But know where to find the answers to questions. Furthermore, every good leader should have a mentor and a mentee throughout the course of their life. A good leader needs a good mentor – anyone else who walked in a similar path – and a mentee to groom to replace them in their absence.

VIBE

Busta Rhymes – **"Put Your Hands Where My Eyes Could See"**
Childish Gambino – **"This is America"**

VICES

Everyone I know has a vice, even babies. Vices can be smoking, video games, food, drugs, porn, work, sex, shopping, hoarding, or people. It's shocking the number of people who are addicted to other people; I've been guilty of this myself. Trauma bonds can be formed for decades before you realize it. At a young age, I was well aware of my vices and of those within my family. So should you. Many people would say I had a drinking problem in high school. In some circles, I was known as the "Cisco Kid." My drink of choice was, of course, "Cisco" a.k.a. "Liquid Crack," followed by some ninety-nine-cent beer as my chaser. However, at the time, I felt the title wasn't warranted because I was an athlete. Of course, I never drank before or on the day of a track meet or football game.

Acknowledging your strengths, weaknesses, vices, and the environment where you come from is vital.

Your environment can affect your growth and alter your trajectory, but it doesn't have to. Recognizing your vices and pitfalls helps you understand the propensity you have to become engaged in such activities. Monitor and manage those vices and surround yourself with those committed to growth. Pray for someone and for yourself.

VIBE

The Notorious B.I.G. – **"Sky's the Limit"**
Drake – **"God's Plan"**
Childish Gambino – **"Redbone"**

IN THE ZONE

As an athlete, student, detective, and coach, being **"in the zone"** is a rare air opportunity, so embrace it. This is the time where you can do no wrong, and it is a difficult time frame to manage because it's "go time." This is the space and chance that will also separate you from your peers. As far as I know, you can't recreate on demand. You can, however, work hard and practice so that you're prepared for your opportunity to be "in the zone." "The zone" is euphoric and life changing. It reinforces your confidence in a way that no speech, person, drug, or alcoholic beverage can duplicate. This is how many people become engulfed with being great. The adrenaline rush is everything.

Being in "the zone" is the feeling of cold blood going through warm veins, the tunnel vision, and the quietness amid chaos. I'm speaking from my own experience and what I have witnessed. I've witnessed Michael Jordan, LeBron James, Kobe Bryant, Vince Carter, Stephen Curry, and the Greek Freak, along with my track athletes' bulging eyes as if they are about to pop out their heads; their flapping cheeks, flexing calf and quad muscles, and veins protruding from the side of their necks as they come around the final corner of the track for the home stretch. They're accelerating while others are not; they're in that rare air space. My athletes consume the rare air you experience when living in the zone. While in the zone, you hear muffled sounds and see very little. However, I'm in my well-known location on the track, and I tell them, "NOW! . . . GO NOW! . . . Finish . . . Finish . . . Turn over . . . Turn over . . . Head down . . . Head down . . . Run downhill . . . Downhill!" They're able to respond with a head nod or shift of the eyes. I'm in the zone with them. There is a shift that takes place in a different gear. You can't believe it because it's never been seen in practice. What is most amazing to me is that in the rare air of the zone, I'm blessed to be able to be present with my athletes in that space—in that gap in time. Because it is in that space where they rarely hear anything and see very little due to tunnel vision, but Coach Chestnut, the "Urban Survivor," was blessed to be present. How lucky am I?

LEAD OR BE LED!

VIBE

The Notorious B.I.G. – **"Hypnotize"**
Drake – **"God's Plan"**

COMPLIMENTS

When given compliments, embrace them and become comfortable being adored. Feel free to compliment others as well as, then watch how it changes someone's entire demeanor. My mother always gave me accolades in public and in private. I cringed. My mother directed me to embrace the positive affirmations, applause, and recognitions because they would soon be needed as armor from the world. We all need those positive reinforcements so that we can resonate with our gifts and accomplishments. As a detective and teacher, I've kept every letter and card given to me from a citizen or student. When I'm not feeling myself or forget that I'm making a difference in this world, I go back and read those kind words. As my mother would say, "It's armor against negative thoughts, mean and negative people, and those who can't see your vision." I urge you not to take compliments, recognitions, and accolades lightly. Embrace them. Read and review cards and positive notes regularly; it's vital reinforcement of your purpose. Life gets tough at times. You will need those words to redirect those times when everything is not going as designed.

VIBE

Snoop Dogg feat. Pharrell Williams – **"Beautiful"**
Raheem DeVaughn – **"I Don't Care"**

KNOW THE DIFFERENCE BETWEEN THE 3 C'S

Many people that you come in contact with have a purpose. For your peace of mind, know the difference between a comrade, constituent, and confidant.

Understand that your comrades are willing to fight for the same things you are fighting for because you have a common goal or enemy. However, they are not your friend, nor will you have long-term interactions.

Your confidant is your "day one," your "ace," your "ride or die." This person is rare in numbers. They are for your benefit and growth.

A constituent will be with you and for you for as long as you represent their issues and desires; they are not your friend either.

Knowing this information and identifying these groups on the front end will allow you to compartmentalize and manage your emotions and expectations.

I quickly learned this lesson when I ran for city council for Clarksville, TN.

VIBE

Kanye West – "**Big Brother**"
TLC – "**What About Your Friends**"

What can I say other than anyone getting prepared to graduate from high school or college should keep *Coach Chestnut's Urban Survivor Notes* in their back pocket or bag. This book can teach them things they usually would not even think of. The book can prepare you for life or help you get through life.

Maceo D.L. Chestnut
Dynamic Middle School Student
and Future Game Changer

UNDERSTAND THE IMPORTANCE OF AUNTS AND UNCLES

Aunts and uncles have a special skill, especially if they were around during your youth. Ask them questions and get their perspectives on life, family, and goals. As someone who has lost both parents, I've found many diamonds in the rough through my aunts and uncles. The support they can supply is genuine. At times, their advice comes across like home cooking, a warm blanket, and the voice of reason.

TAP IN!

VIBE

Sly and the Family Stone – **"Family Affair"**

CURVE THEM LIKE THEY CURVE YOU

When people do what's best for them, make sure you do what's best for you. Actions will always speak louder than words. Listen to the background in music, movies, and real life. Assume nothing, take nothing for granted, seek clarification, read between the lines when needed, and trust your instincts. You must learn to protect your peace as soon as possible. This is a learned skill over time. However, when doing what's best for you, be humble in your actions and with your tongue because it's nothing personal; it's just self-preservation. Move in ways that are effective and decisive, not bitter. This is essential in a workplace, budding relationship, or business setting. This is not to say that when you start doing what's best for you, others won't get offended, but that's not your business.

Before I legally divorced my wife, it was already done in my mind. Regardless of what transpired between us, rarely did it faze me.

VIBE

Rick Ross – **"Ashton Martin Music"**
Drake & Jay-Z – **"Pound Cake"**
Sade – **"Soldier of Love"**

JUST BECAUSE YOU'RE WORKING HARD DOES NOT MEAN YOU'RE WORKING EFFICIENTLY

Make sure you are aware of your time and progress. Manage your time as if it was money.

Time is the rare commodity we assume we have a lot of.

It was August 13th at roughly 10:20 a.m. I was in the middle of teaching investigative tactics and techniques to my students at the West Creek Criminal Justice and Homeland Security Academy when my classroom phone rang. My sister Sheila's voice was cracking and somber. "Mone, if you wanna say goodbye to mom, get here fast. Hurry up, Mone." I called my daughter, Sadaija, and told her we had to roll to Buffalo. I told my brother, Brian, to pack. I would be there within the hour. One hour later, my daughter called and said, "Dad, I'm rollin'." I was on the road about forty-five minutes after her. Four hours into my 750-mile trek from Tennessee to Buffalo, my sister called back screaming, "Mone, she's gone! Mone, mom is gone!" My brother, Leonard, jumped on the phone, "Mone, you okay?" A whimpered "yes" was all I could muster. My brother, Brian, sat next to me in my Nissan Maxima, rolling at 85 mph+, and said, "She gone, ain't she?" I responded, "Yup." Since that day, that's all I had in me. I was no longer a "grown man." I regressed to a little boy whose hero was gone. I loved that woman so much that every keystroke is like a dagger into my heart as I convey this message. Time waits for no one.

VIBE

Kevin Gates – **"I Don't Get Tired"**
Gucci Mane feat. Migos – **"I Get the Bag"**

DREAM

Dream so big that what you want seems impossible. Don't concern yourself with who failed at it before you. Focus on who has made it before you. Furthermore, if it's never been done, then you're on your way to being a trailblazer. Surround yourself with movers and shakers. Illustrate a "can-do" attitude and seek those who are doing what you want to do. Ironically, most of what I dreamed of has come true, and in some cases, they have exceeded my expectations even after I thought I was dreaming big enough. Also, don't concern yourself with comparing your dreams and visions to those of others. Your journey is uniquely your own.

VIBE

The Game – **"Dreams"**
Nas – **"One Mic"**
Kanye West – **"Through the Wire"**
Kanye West – **"Jesus Walks"**

CHEAT CODE

Your cheat code is your go-to move to get yourself back on track when you have been derailed by life. Everybody needs a cheat code for self-preservation; it aids you in getting back on your perch. When you are triggered by something or have failed at something, what's your go-to plan of action?

I have a series of actions as my cheat codes:

1) I get a haircut/beard trim.
2) I wear a new outfit.
3) I take a long car ride.
4) I listen to a heavy dose of Jay-Z, Nas, Tupac, and The Notorious B.I.G.
5) I binge-watch stand-up comedy shows.

The next thing you know, I'm back on the rails and moving forward.

VIBE

Khalid feat. Ari Lennox – **"Scenic Drive"**

POWER COLOR

Every good Urban Survivor must know their power color. It's different for everyone. Your power color must have the ability to instantaneously shift your mindset. Your power color is a freshly recharged battery on your back. Your power color puts a smile on your face. Your power color says, "I know I'm ready for whatever, whenever, and however."

My power color is blood red. In fact, no other shade of red will do. Unquestionably, when I'm in blood red, I know that I'm prepared for whatever, whenever, and however. Blood red is actually another cheat code all by itself.

VIBE

Mary J. Blige feat. Grand Puba – **"What's the 411?"**

BOOKS BUILD MINDS

Regardless of whether you are an avid reader or not, always keep a good book with you. This is crucial when traveling. Even if you don't read it regularly, a book will make stagnant time seem timeless and redirect any annoyance that may occur in your travels. Two books I had zero intentions of reading were the autobiography of Earl Simmons aka DMX and an urban love story called *Sweet St. Louis*. Both books kept my attention until I completed them. Keeping a book on me at all times was great advice my mother gave me.

VIBE

Nas – **"If I Ruled the World"**

MULTITASKING MAKES IT MESSY

As hard as this may be to believe, multitasking usually does not bring out the best results. Your best results will usually come when you are laser focused on the task at hand. This is true whether the task is work or investing in a budding relationship.

VIBE

Fugees – **"Killing Me Softly with His Song"**

INSPIRATIONAL RESPONSIBILITY

When you have a group of people who believe in you, are invested in you, support you, and cheer for your success, don't let them down.

The main reason ***Coach Chestnut's Urban Survivor Notes*** was created is because I owe it to my grandmother, parents, children, and students. How could I disappoint or let any of these beautiful humans down?

VIBE

Lauryn Hill – **"Everything is Everything"**

TAXES

Most people I know cringe when they see or hear the word "taxes" or even the word "math." As a high school student, I was honestly scared of math, but I liked money. I'm not the type of person who just likes to earn money by working for an hourly wage. I love the challenge of buying something that I actually like, then using it, making it better, and having the ability to sell it for more than what I invested into it. My niche is real estate, where I've proven my ability to make a profit in some of the most unorthodox ways. When you operate and finesse like I do, taxes will be a sobering reality to all your financial gains. Each year, I ran to some tax preparer and accountant, giving them total control over my finances and taxes and providing little input. As of today, I'm not sure if I was ever taken advantage of because I never properly monitored my finances closely enough. Fortunately, I wasn't making enough money to really cause a financial dilemma, but I had to acknowledge this oversight. Prior to my thirty-fourth birthday, I decided never to allow another person to have access to my finances until I had reviewed them first. Whether it's business or personal, know your business before anyone else does.

Make your money, save your money, enjoy your money, and have your money make more money. Most importantly, make the money; don't let it make you.

Platforms like TurboTax and QuickBooks can empower you to stay up on your business before you give access to anyone else. If you're working a nine-to-five, side hustle, or have a small business, do your own taxes first.

VIBE

Cardi B – **"Money"**

SEX

The act of sex is a powerful drug. Be aware of the good, the bad, and the ugly that comes with sexual intercourse. Sexual desires will affect your entire life for the rest of your life. Believe the people who are sexually active and have caused another person to say to you, "If I can't have you, no one will."

In my most humbled opinion, sexual intercourse is just as addictive as crack cocaine, heroin, cigarettes, and alcohol.

Sexual intercourse will have you involved with the wrong person far longer than you need to be just to get a "fix." Sex will have you planning your entire work schedule around the act of sex. Sex will cause you to be late for work and miss doctor appointments. Sex has even inspired me to drive 1,600 miles for a day's worth of pleasure, then justify my actions. Choose your sexual partners wisely by having an understanding of the context of the sexual relationship so that you don't misinterpret its intentions.

I've had serious conversations with my father about sex and relationships that quickly changed how I carried myself in this area. There are two conversations my father and I had that stood out the most. As a man, I'm lucky that my father had the courage to be brutally honest about his intentions, actions, and his truth.

My father told me that although I was not a mistake, my arrival definitely was not planned, nor did he want any more kids after me. However, once I was born and started walking, talking, asking questions, and inquiring about who *he* was as a person, he knew I was special. To his own admission, he had no idea what to do with a child like me other than occupy my time by putting me to work. Furthermore, he knew he lacked the ability to properly express love for another person because he was never taught that himself. He did, however, have the ability to express himself to specific women that he loved. The caveat to that was that he had the charisma to express to women that he had needs and that he believed they had the same needs. With that being established, he suggested that both parties should express their sexual needs and wants. Then, they should focus on achieving those wants and needs as one at their convenience! Might I add my father only had a sixth-grade education. Nonetheless, he was a scholar in his own right.

As simple and direct as my father's ideology was, those instructions and views are emotional. They are vibes and energies that will not flourish in the long term. Never forget, there is a difference between someone having love for you and being in love with you.

Consume that emotionally and intellectually as you see fit.

VIBE

Trey Songz - **"On Call"**
Slick Rick – **"Hey Young World"**
LL Cool J – **"I Need Love"**
Biz Markie – **"Just a Friend"**
Jay Z & Beanie Sigel – **"Where Have You Been"**
Beanie Sigel feat. Jay Z & Young Rell – **"Still Got Love for You"**
Jay-Z – **"Soon You'll Understand"**

DISTRACTIONS

Distractions come in all shapes and sizes. Many are self-inflicted. Some are meant to challenge your purpose. The ability to be aware is key in these situations. Knowing which things need to be completed and which things are optional are the boundaries that define your actions. Regardless of the type of distraction, reinforce for yourself what things you must get done. Everything isn't optional.

VIBE

DMX – **"Ready to Meet Him"**
DMX feat. Regina Bell – **"Angel"**
FKJ & Masego – **"Tadow"**

PROCRASTINATION STOPS PROGRESSION

Procrastination is the greatest reason why our visions die with us. The ideology that time is on our side and we have plenty of time to accomplish our goals and aspirations is ludicrous. I have had to accept the fact that my parents will never witness the release of ***Coach Chestnut's Urban Survivor Notes*** simply because I procrastinated.

VIBE

Meek Mill feat. Diddy – **"Cold Hearted"**

DRUGS

As the youngest of thirteen children, nine of my siblings struggled with drug and alcohol addiction. Notice I said "addiction" because if they could have quit abusing drugs, they would have. However, when you are aware of the crack epidemic in America's inner cities, you're knowledgeable enough to not judge everyone for the demons they fight. Nonetheless I have witnessed how drugs and alcohol can destroy an entire family bloodline. I have been told so many times by addicts, "I just wanted to try it to see what it was like." One of my siblings disclosed that from the first time they tried crack cocaine, they have been trying to stop. I was introduced to and provided with marijuana at a young age. Accessibility has never been an issue. I was so young that I assumed it was a rite of passage. It was a challenge to keep my mouth shut to my parents, and a challenge to handle that high of THC like a champ even as it perverted my lungs. Recover and act normal was the play.

Although I experimented as a teenager, I never developed the need to consume the substances on a regular basis because I've never liked being controlled by anything or anyone. Shit, I was my own man at a young age but still a little boy drinking Kool-Aid and crying about having to eat Brussels sprouts. Emotionally, I've seen how drug addiction broke the spirit of my mother as she saw her babies suffering. My mom was forced to watch her children being stripped of everything she invested into them. She cleaned the homes of attorneys and judges on her hands and knees to earn extra money for proper legal representation, jail books, and care packages. The children from her womb slept in correctional facilities and rehabilitation centers as they fought for their independence from narcotics, gambling, and alcohol. My father worked sixteen to eighteen hours a day in a steel mill to maintain a home not owned by the government so that my siblings and I could have a better vision of how to make a living.

In today's ever-changing urban slang and jargon we call that "securing the bag." However, I now know how to account for the front end, back end, and identify my residuals. My experiences are not exclusive to me, but experienced by youth around the globe. Many have similar stories like mine, but are too ashamed and embarrassed to have these tough, but necessary, conversations. Fortunately, the Grand Architect of the Universe already had a plan for me, as flawed as I am, to empower youth in the most authentic way. It's taken me forty-eight years to construct this manuscript for human consumption. After being an educator and track & field coach, working with today's youth for the past twenty years was confirmation of the need for ***Coach Chestnut's Urban Survivor Notes***.

VIBE

Grandmaster Flash & The Furious Five – **"The Message"**

HUGS ARE POWERFUL

I've never been the most affectionate person, but I'm learning. One day, I went to visit a female friend. Upon entering her home, we embraced, and seconds later, I attempted to pull away. She clutched and tightened her hug, then held the embrace much longer than I was interested in or was even comfortable with. However, recently, I have come to understand and embrace the power of the hug. But the power must be met with proper hygiene and sincerity. In some cases, a transfer of energy is even possible and provides the ability to heal.

I remember running into a long-time Army comrade and embracing her. I noticed her hug was not the norm . . . and we ended up exchanging numbers. Three days later, I still thought about the hug, so I called her and asked, "Do you hug everyone like you hugged me?" She replied, "That hug was a clear, concise message to let you know what I wanted and nothing less." So, I sent a message as well, standing strong in what I was capable of, which we discussed after breakfast the next morning.

VIBE

Maze feat. Frankie Beverly – **"Happy Feelings"**

THE PIVOT

When life begins to make you uncomfortable and easily agitated about your vibe, energy, and environment, the pivot begins. Many of us have ignored the signs as we've gotten older, but as toddlers, we sought what relieved and comforted us. We became picky about the clothes we wore, the food we ate, and the people we allowed to hold us.

After graduating high school, I enrolled in Buffalo State College where I was supposed to report for spring training football camp. Needless to say, I did not report. I had no drive or interest anymore. I liked playing football, but I didn't love it. I quickly realized I disliked being in pain for two to three days after a game. Number #42 of the Bennett Tigers was my brand at the time. I was the left outside-linebacker. Skeet and I locked the left side down, so head-on collisions were the norm.

Playing football and running track were a way of life at the prestigious Lewis J. Bennett High School in Buffalo, NY. I focused my attention on preparing for the upcoming track season while working two jobs and with my father for his landscaping business. At that time, I realized I had a place to live, plenty of money, and multiple female companions. At age seventeen, I was winning. However, something inside screamed, "I need more! I want more!" So, I joined the United States Army and served eight years, three months, and twenty-five days in the Quartermaster Corps. However, I was a divorced single parent raising a daughter, so I needed to pivot toward establishing a proper home and lifestyle for Sadaija. In this process, my hobby of coaching track pivoted to a new coaching career. Simultaneously, I established myself as a proven professional as criminal investigator, working cases in the areas of child sex abuse, homicide, and assistant commander of the crisis negotiations team. After thirteen years, the universe spoke to me again by pushing me to elevate, so I became a criminal justice instructor, which allowed me the most growth mentally, physically, emotionally, financially, and most importantly, intellectually. Eight years after feeling accomplished, I sold my brand-new home, packed up my truck, and relocated to Washington, D.C.

When it's time to pivot, it will be difficult to ignore. When you pivot, be prepared for bullcrap and blessings because both will be present.

VIBE

SZA – **"Good Days"**
Janet Jackson – **"Any Time, Any Place"**

HATE - HURT - HONOR

Relationships can be complex, whether it's with a family member, spouse, or significant other; be sure to identify their purpose in your life. After you've identified their purpose and passion, when you share trials and triumphs of your own, pay close attention to their response compared to your own. Then ask yourself whether they are reciprocating HATE, HURT, OR HONOR and then handle that relationship accordingly.

VIBE

Burna Boy – **"Last Last"**
Yo Gotti – **"More Ready Than Ever"**
Meek Mill – **"Dreams and Nightmares"**

RULES ARE MERELY GUIDELINES

When you are on your grind and trying to accomplish your goals, don't allow rules to stop you. Rules are for those who are willing to accept a "no" instead of trying to acquire a "yes". Rules are not laws; therefore, they are negotiable. They don't apply to everyone. My older brother, Spoon, always said to me, "Do not accept a 'no' from someone who can't authorize a 'yes'". I've lived by that religiously.

VIBE

The Notorious B.I.G. – **"Ten Crack Commandments"**
DMX – **"Who We Be"**

CLOSED MOUTHS DON'T GET FED

You must be willing to have tough conversations even if you are the focal point. Also, have the courage to confront someone who will become the focal point because of their actions or a lack of action. These conversations can be based on a plethora of subject matters from politics, sex, money, elected officials, personal hygiene, and finances. Be honest and candid during these tough conversations because clarity is the key to progress.

My parents gave me an open invitation to talk about anything as long as my conversation was in a respectful manner. My father was brutally honest about every subject matter.

VIBE

DMX – **"We Right Here"**
Soul II Soul – **"Keep It Movin'"**

HURT, NOT HATE

At some point in your life, you'll meet someone, but the relationship will not work out, no matter how bad you try to make it work. Hopefully, you will part on good terms and possibly even keep in contact with one another. I've had a situation or two where this has been the case. With one particular ex-girlfriend, after some time, we were periodically able to share in each other's growth. She shared her goals and accomplishments with me, and I essentially cheered her on. However, when I did the same, it was interpreted as if I was bragging. Over some period of time, I got confused about this energy. Then, in another interaction, she mentioned how it was "very funny that I did not do certain things while we dated," and I was actually offended. Right then, I knew all her previous actions and reactions came from a place of hurt, not hate. Whenever possible, identify the source of the vibe and energy you receive from those who are supposedly on your team.

VIBE

Jhené Akio – **"Happiness Over Everything"**
Meek Mill – **"Flamerz Flow"**

NEW YOU, NEW ME

In life, you have to learn to meet people where they are and believe what you see more than what you hear.

One year, you could be in what seems to be a sound, peaceful relationship yet feel completely unsatisfied and stagnate. You and your significant other could no longer be invested in one another. You could be afraid to try new things, go to new places, speak your truth in fear of hurting someone's feelings, or adopt a lone-wolf mentality.

A relationship could be over instantaneously because one, if not both, parties have just given up. The love may even still be present, but the will to fight for one another has evaporated. Two years later, you could meet someone who matches your energy, finishes your sentences, seeks to understand you, develops long-term and mutual goals, and motivates you professionally and personally. They make it clear that they want to do life with you and have a front-row seat for your trials and triumphs. All of sudden, you're traveling the world, trying new foods, jumping out of perfectly good planes, and smiling without notice. Then, you wonder why "this thing," this "vibe," or "energy," couldn't be discovered sooner in life with someone who desired you as much as you desired them. Different people bring out different energies and vibes. Some pray for such a connection. Then, when it's presented to them, they run or sabotage every aspect of the situation.

This is why you gotta accept and meet people where they are, then decide if this is for your betterment.

VIBE

Lil Duval – "**Smile (Living My Best Life)**"

FLAWS AND FREEDOM

The sooner you accept your flaws, the sooner you become free of what society thinks you should look like, act like, and be like. The key is to focus on becoming the best version of yourself while continuing to be your most authentic self, and the universe will shift towards you. You will only need to pivot when there's bad weather!

VIBE

Beyonce – **"Flaws and All"**
Juice WRLD – **"Flaws and Sins"**
Tory Lanez – **"P.A.I.N."**

"QUIT MOMENT"

Do not succumb to the moment when the universe gives you the opportunity to give in and give up in the midst of your challenge, goal, destiny, and most important, dreams. The "quit moment" is always lingering, but at times, its presence is attention seeking. Move forward and stay focused on your intended outcome. Think of the glory and confidence that comes with setting a plan, manifesting it, then executing it. Only then can the world no longer ignore you, and this new you that has been born.

The "quit moment" is the cause of the best ideas being buried with some of the most talented individuals!

VIBE

LL Cool J – **"I'm Bad"**
RUN DMC – **"It's Tricky"**
Lumidee feat. Busta Rhymes – **"Never Leave You"**

MAINTAIN YOUR STANDARDS

Between maturing in your business, career, relationships, commitments, and contractual bonds, you must maintain your standards. Once you have compromised your standard, it's almost impossible to restore them. Even if someone despises you, they still respect that you remained your most authentic self in spite of issues.

VIBE

The Game feat. 50 Cent – **"Hate It or Love It"**

FORESIGHT

Foresight is the ability to predict or the action of predicting what will happen or be needed in the future. **The best way to improve your foresight is to question your assumptions, acknowledge your own bias, and question your gut instinct.** You must also know the past and understand how history is not only illustrated but depicted. Most importantly, be in constant contact with young adults.

Having foresight has provided me the opportunity to be financially stable, removed me from toxic relationships, and provided for my children and my parents. Foresight is essential to becoming wealthy and the greatest version of yourself.

In 2016, I invested in a vacant lot in a neighborhood that was considered blighted, but I saw its potential. Also, I love real estate, so I had foresight and knowledge on real estate in the city of Clarksville, TN. After the cost, taxes, and fees, I paid a little less than $10K cash for the vacant lot. It is now worth six times what I paid for it.

FORESIGHT!

VIBE

Gunna feat. Lil Baby – **"Blindfold"**
Jay-Z – **"The Story of O.J."**

PROGRESSION OVER PERFECTION

It will never be the right time. Just get started and keep it moving. The perfect day, year, or situation will never come, so make your move.

I once tried to wait for the perfect time to date this woman so that I could eventually marry her. In fact, I found out I was not alone. Other men, and even teenage boys, have had this ideology. None of us knew that the "best" time would never come. I'm not saying that you should always "live in the moment," either. However, a calculated risk can be shelved only for so long. Personally, the woman and I have dated others over the years, so we're now both so jaded that we don't have the confidence to even date each other anymore.

Hey, but y'all grown. Do what . . . you've been doing.

VIBE

SZA – **"The Weekend"**
Lil Baby – **"The Bigger Picture"**

YOUR GIFT

Everyone has a gift, and that gift can change your life. Seek to discover the gift that you and everyone on earth are here to share with the world, regardless of race, color, or creed.

Ask yourself, "Now that I know my gift, what do I want to do with it?"

VIBE

Ledesi – **"Lose Control"**

A GOOD LIFE IS EXPENSIVE

Prepare yourself for the "good life" because it's going to cost you the "bad life" where there are no coupons or discounts.

The perfect example is when you look at the price of organic unprocessed foods compared to processed foods. Essentially, fresh fruit is more expensive than candy.

The "good life" is expensive. Eat and live well. Smile often.

VIBE

Kem – **"Share My Life"**
Chrisette Michele – **"A Couple of Forevers"**

BEING A PARENT IS NOT A LIFESTYLE

When you decide to have unprotected sex, you're also consenting to having a child and assuming the risk of giving or getting a sexually transmitted disease.

Being a parent is not a lifestyle. It's agreeing to take care of another human being far beyond what you're obligated to. As a parent, you're putting your needs aside for many years so that your child can blossom into a great citizen. Being a parent is one of the greatest acts of kindness and selflessness.

Furthermore, popping Plan B pills is not a safe or long-term form of birth control, nor are the various "pull out" methods.

VIBE

DJ Jazzy Jeff & the Fresh Prince – **"Parents Just Don't Understand"**

SUPPLY DICTATES DEMAND

The more accessible you are to the masses, the less in demand you may become. This means that you do not need to be in every club or at social events every day of the week. Maintain your exclusivity. Keep the audience intrigued. Keep your demand high so that you can serve your supply at your leisure.

VIBE

Jodeci – **"Forever My Lady"**

EXCLUSIVITY RAISES THE VALUE

Just like supply and demand impacts the price of goods, being exclusive about who you allow to experience you separates you from your peers. Obtain some skill, service, or experience that people can only get from you! People must contact you and go through you to have the experience they seek. Remember, today's price is not yesterday's price, so govern yourself accordingly.

VIBE

Jagged Edge – **"I Gotta Be"**
Nas – **"You Owe Me"**

YOU CAN'T SAVE EVERYONE

Many times in life, you must do what's best for you without concerning yourself about the needs of others. You may feel guilty in the process, but it's key to your growth to move forward. Before I left for the military, I put all romantic relationships aside and tied up all loose ends in the streets. If it was meant to be, we would reconnect. That was my philosophy.

VIBE

Jay-Z – Mary J. Blige – **"Can't Knock the Hustle"**
James Brown – **"It's a Man's World"**

CONSTRUCTIVE CRITICISM BUILDS CHARACTER

You must be willing to receive what you may need to hear about yourself. But if you are willing to accept or even effectively listen to constructive criticism, your growth will be immeasurable.

One day I asked my daughter, "Am I really a good dad? Have I done what you needed me to do for you?" Sadaija, in return, said, "Yes, dad, you've done a great job. You've always made sure I had everything I needed. Also, you never missed any important events or milestones. You've fallen asleep during some events, but you were present."

So now with my son, I make sure I don't fall asleep as much.

VIBE

Total – **"Can't You See"**
Terrence Howard (*Hustle & Flow*) – **"It's Hard Out Here for a Pimp"**

YOUR LIFESTYLE VS. YOUR CAREER

Decide on the lifestyle you desire, then design your career choice around it. I believe this process is the key to achieving the work-life balance you need and it will help you manage stress. Unfortunately, I never really considered my "lifestyle" part of my process of adulting. It was only when I found myself overwhelmed, underpaid, and not appreciated that I made this a priority. After dating a simplistic woman who cared nothing about anything materialistic, I began to understand and invest in my "lifestyle." While being a police detective, educator, and track coach, I neglected taking care of my personal time and did not apply myself enough when working out at the gym. Making a decision about your lifestyle is so important. The money, homes, and jewels mean nothing if you can't enjoy them. Currently, I live in a city where I don't necessarily need to take a vacation to "get away" because my current lifestyle doesn't need a vacation, per se. I just need to see new things, visit new locations, and experience new cultures.

VIBE

Young Thug & Rich Homie Quan – **"Lifestyle"**

MAKE YOUR OWN LANE

Previously, I spoke about supply and demand, exclusivity, your name is your brand, and being resourceful. Well, due to technology and the availability of knowledge at your fingertips, there is no need for anyone to feel stuck.

Make your own lane, create your own buzz word, and change the game to fit your vision. Become the wave, dictate the pace, lock in the cadence, provide the vision, then dominate the competition.

Do good business and be kind to people.

VIBE

Yo Gotti feat. Rich Homie Quan - **"I Know"**
The Notorious B.I.G. – **"Notorious Thugs"**

COUNT ON YOURSELF!

You are your best friend and your own cheerleader. Your goals and dreams are your responsibility, and you do not have the right to think another human will know and understand your journey. No other person but you can really see your vision, which is why you have to spend some time to try to convey your message.

Beware of starting a business and expecting family members to support it or believing they will keep you afloat until the business takes off. Your dreams and goals do not care about what someone else did or did not do. Shut up and hustle harder.

If you gotta cut people off, do it. If you gotta put yourself on punishment, do it.

Dream, plan, manifest, execute, then dominate.

VIBE

Boosie Badazz feat. Rich Homie Quan – **"Like a Man"**

MOST REWARDING JOBS WILL COST TIME AND NOT PAY WELL

When you choose a career that involves helping others, understand it may be the most rewarding. But many times, social service professionals are not properly compensated. You must be OK with this and accept the unique opportunity you have to improve the livelihood of another person who probably can't do anything for you.

VIBE

K Camp – **"What's on Your Mind"**

MOMENTS IN THE MOMENT

Some things should not have a video or a picture to recall the moment. Sometimes, you should live in the moment and embrace the experience.

You ever notice how most "guy trips" or "homeboy getaways" rarely have pictures?

Most of the time, men live in the moment. Our memories are photographic.

VIBE

Dej Loaf – **"Try Me"**

QUALITY YOU CAN AFFORD

When it's time to buy furniture, clothes, cars, and houses, always go for quality the first time. If your funds and finances are not ready, wait. Do not buy cars you know are no good, furniture you have to put together, or a home where the neighborhood has zero potential. When your money is tight, focus on coordinating everything. Avoid fads, stick with traditional, and add to it. Take that dress or new suit, ball that fabric up in your hand, then let it drop. Does it look like a bag of chips balled up, or did it drop back to its original form? Quality garments will always retreat back to their original form.

VIBE

Mooski – **"Track Star"**
Tupac – **"Picture Me Rollin'"**

WINNERS . . . WIN

Every person I know that has success in their chosen area would be just as successful if they needed to shift because winners always win! You gotta have a winning temperament and ideology. Have intertwined cockiness and confidence; but stay humble. I love being around winners, the cream of the crop, and the all-stars. It elevates my prowess and cognitive skills. Being around winners is stimulating and necessary.

As a track coach for over twenty years, I was exposed to winners on a daily basis. It was the best environment to exist in.

VIBE

Wale – **"Lotus Flower Bomb"**

BE DANGEROUS

Don't be so nice that you're not on your game or out here playing the victim. Be dangerous.

They say, "If you stay ready, then you don't have to get ready." My mother would say, "It's better to have and not need than to need and not have."

VIBE

Nas – **"Hate Me Now"**

GO TO WEDDINGS

Attending weddings provides new content for your mind. I attended the wedding of one my former track and cross-country runners. As I entered the venue, I asked Tevin, "Are you ready?" He responded, "Yes, sir. I'm ready to spend the rest of my life with her." Tevin's smile could illuminate an entire sanctuary. As the wedding event proceeded, I noticed Tevin's bride had the same big smile, and her eyes were always on Tevin. Once the ceremony was over, I noticed how Tevin kept at least one hand on his new wife at all times. Whenever Tevin had to let go of his new wife, she would then place her hand on him.

Love wins again!

VIBE

Jagged Edge – **"Let's Get Married"**

OLD STANDARDS VS. NEW BEGINNINGS

When you venture into new cities and relationships, you cannot apply all your old standards and tactics to your new beginnings. Life waits on no one to catch up, so you must move with the times to function properly in your new beginnings.

Plan for the future. Live in the moment. Flourish in your new beginnings.

VIBE

Jagged Edge feat. Nelly – **"Where the Party At"**
Tupac – **"Lord Knows"**

RACE CARD

If you decide to date outside your race, you must be resilient to the pressures of society, especially if you decide to engage in conversations on the subject matter. Dating outside your race in itself, can be difficult, especially when your own friends and family members dislike it.

Hopefully, you have a little petty in you so that the opinions of your family and friends monitor and manage themselves accordingly!

In my lifetime, I've only had one serious adult relationship where I've dated outside my race. The entire time, I felt like I was cheating on every black woman in America, which is something I've only shared with a select few people. Furthermore, I don't believe this feeling is exclusive to me. I've paid attention to how people who date outside their race act and react to specific situations.

VIBE

Paul McCartney and Stevie Wonder – **"Ebony and Ivory"**
Tupac – **"Only God Can Judge Me"**

PROCRASTINATION

Identify your distractions and discord. Typically, we procrastinate when we must get things done that we really don't want to do.

Reduce your distractions and control your procrastination.

VIBE

Stevie Wonder – **"That Girl"**

FIRE

Never take what is said in the heat of a verbal argument as gospel. But don't forget what is said either. Many things are said when a person is angry.

When you are hungry, horny, or heated, avoid important conversations until these issues are addressed.

VIBE

Alicia Keys feat. Maxwell – **"Fire We Make"**

DOLLA BILL

My father once told me that women love to buy gifts, cook meals, and motivate the men in their lives. However, no woman he has ever met likes to physically put money in a man's hand. They would rather leave it on a kitchen table, on a nightstand, or in the visor of a car than place that money in his hand.

My dad said to avoid this type of situation whenever possible.

VIBE

James Brown – **"It's a Man's World"**

G.I.

Don't get comfortable with any type of government contract job, benefits, program, or subsidy. The government is focused on the government. Of course, you should utilize government assistance to recover and get back on your feet. But after that, stand tall on your own. Be in control of your trajectory and avoid being part of some yearly government statistical data.

VIBE

N.W.A. – **"Straight Outta Compton"**
Tupac – **"Against All Odds"**

HOOD LOVE

The hood will never love you like you've loved it! In fact, it's impossible because it was not designed for anyone to succeed. The hood is a place to exist, to labor, grow old, then die off. I say get out of the hood, then buy up the hood, and be a part of the rebuilding of the hood. But never look for love in the hood or in a person that was not designed to love you back.

VIBE

Mary J. Blige feat. Trey Songz – **"We Got Hood Love"**

BEGGING

No one likes to feel like they are begging when it comes to asking for help. If you ever feel like you are begging for anything for any reason, remove yourself. More importantly, your removal must be executed with high veracity.

You can't keep anyone who doesn't want to be kept.

VIBE

Wyclef Jean feat. Mary J. Blige – **"911"**

STEPPARENTS

If you have a stepparent in your life and they are honestly doing their very best for you, give them a break. The position of a stepparent is a lonely situation, with all of the responsibilities of a biological parent. Every stepparent is just waiting for the day when the child makes the infamous statement heard all around the world, "You ain't my daddy!" or "You ain't my mother!" It's like stuffing your nose with hot brussels sprouts and dipping your eyelids in bleach.

In my travels, I was invited to hang out at Legacy 5 Lounge in South Euclid, Ohio. While there, my daughter's stepfather persuaded me to order the "Soul Rolls" and I was in heaven. I've become really cool with him over the years. I'm directly aware of the difficult position he holds, but we make it happen. Furthermore, as men, we have the best interest of all the children within our circles. We've both supported or empowered each other's children without expectations and more from our convictions.

VIBE

Slick Rick – **"Hey Young World"**
Kanye w/Jay-Z – **"Never Let Me Down"**

The statement "survival of the fittest" is one of the oldest theories of evolution used to explain how something best adjusted to its environment will be the most successful at surviving. How can we evolve if we do not observe and learn what it takes to survive? Coach Chestnut has not only been a track coach and educator to me, but a life coach long after I left his classroom. He has taught me that survival in our lifetime does not just depend on money and having a certain career. All physical, mental, and emotional aspects influence your life trajectory. The wisdom, inspiration, and experience in this book can highlight life's complications in their truest forms, without faltering and in authenticity. His own observations and life history delineate his hard work, showing his ability to acquire knowledge through learning and growth. With this, his personal experiences are the best explanations to a philosophy for not only surviving, but prospering.

CAITLIN DUNCAN
Former Student Athlete

HEROES

Growing up, everyone had their superheroes on television; I lived with mine.

My brother Sherman was always on the move, traveling up and down the East Coast. I admired the freedom he had. My brother Leonard had the biggest impact on me because I literally wanted to be just like him. Leonard definitely showed me how to make it in the streets. Everyone else in the streets talked about dollars; Leonard spoke in percentages and raffled off numbers like a calculator. This negro was soaked in confidence and never gave the impression that he was scared of anything. My brother Brian gave me the desire to learn and get things done on your own by any means necessary. Even if you didn't have the money, talk your way into or out of the issue. My brother Timmy was so resilient; he battled his addictions and fought to free himself. I believe I witnessed him go through withdrawal at one time as he fought himself, vomited, screamed, cried, then slept hard. He beat the demon that day, and I was so proud of him. I visited him in jail, at rehab, and at every program he completed to get back on his feet. I was there whenever and wherever because I knew he needed to see family so he could continue to fight the good fight.

My brother Darrell was like the family enforcer. You just did not want to mess with any of us. Darrell would tell you to your face, "I will kill yo a**, football head," and no one doubted that. As a young kid, I always felt protected and insulated. I never had a reason to feel scared. It was so empowering not to be scared about anything going on in life because I had brothers and sisters that protected me. This allowed me to learn and understand myself as a person at a young age. I had a front-row seat to all my siblings' lives because I was the youngest, and it was never a dull moment.

The other family enforcer was my brother Sheldon, who was an actual martial arts competitor. He also provided a safety net and always drove my latest purchased vehicle when I came into town and slept on his couch. Many times when I drove from Tennessee to Buffalo, I went to Sheldon's house to get some sleep before I engaged with the rest of the family. My brother Terry was one of the best-dressed dudes and had a record collection second to none. He drove a manual transmission Volkswagen Beetle with the Rolls Royce front and white-walled tires. He once came to one of my football games in that car dressed in a shark-gray suit. I could've sworn the negro was walking on water.

My brother Darren was the computer expert in the family. In fact, he was before his time as far as technology. My sister Lelani was my dad's prize. The rule was he better not find out something had happened to her. Lelani is such a natural leader; she basically was in charge of us and still is in many ways.

My sister Sheila is no joke. You're going to be a man in her presence even if you're only half a man. She has also taken all her trials and tribulations head-on. When it came to the death of our mother, she held it down for everyone when everyone assumed she would be an emotional mess. Nah, "B," my sister stood tall like a soldier in formation.

My brother Jeff, aka "Spoon," was my room dog growing up, and in many ways, he was like a father figure because sometimes we were all we had. Jeff was one of the first multi-sport athletes I had ever seen. He played football, basketball, baseball, hockey, bowling, 8-ball, and even ping-pong. We weren't really poor growing up—just broke as hell. Just enough money came in the house to keep the lights on and food in the fridge. When I was seven years old and Jeff was eleven, I told Jeff, "We're going to do something different. We're not going to keep living like this." Jeff responded in a tone as if he believed every word I said at that very moment, and I felt it. I was ready at age seven. I felt it. I knew it. I dreamed it. I just didn't know what "it" was.

All my sisters-in-law, brother-in-law, uncles, and aunts were hands-on with me. Many had great careers not even mentioned these days. In my family, I had electricians, plant foremen, medical staff, property owners, business owners, and military personnel. These are, and always have been, my heroes—the people I looked up to. These are the men and women that hold me accountable. They want nothing but the best for me and ask nothing from me.

Make sure you have some tangible heroes in your life . . . your real life.

VIBE

Sister Sledge – **"We Are Family"**
Frankie Beverly and Maze – **"Before I Let You Go"**
DMX – **"Look Thru My Eyes"**

EPILOGUE

First and foremost, I hope this work is received in the way I prayed it to be. This work is not meant to be the end all be all. Even more, it is a cheat code for youth and young adults, a reminder for older adults, a starting point to establish dialogue between parents and their children, and a reference point between generations and genders. Empowering youth is the key to success for society and to keeping all of us youthful. I hope this work makes my siblings proud, my children stronger and wiser, and my family members aware of our potential and greatness. I hope this work provides every student and athlete I've ever come in contact with a better understanding of why I asked so much of them. To those students and athletes: I tried to treat you as if you were my own biological child. I ran for councilman for the city of Clarksville, TN, solely for you to have sidewalks, city bus transportation, city bus shelters, and a new community center on the north side. The beauty of that is my children saw and took part in that process. My son passed out flyers and knocked on doors in the blistering heat at eight years old because he wanted to see his dad and the youth of Clarksville win.

That's empowerment. That's love.

Respectfully,
Coach DeMone A. Chestnut
LEAD OR BE LED

CPSIA information can be obtained
at www.ICGtesting.com
Printed in the USA
LVHW071829260323
742630LV00010B/283

9 798985 978018